To Anne

Lasso the West in Art

M Fellows

A Handshake is Enough

The Cowboy Way Through Art and Poetry

MARLESS FELLOWS

Written By

LESLIE V. BAY

Publisher:
Marless Fellows
6140 E. Cave Creek Road, Suite 3B
Cave Creek, AZ 85331

Email: artbymarless@hotmail.com
www.saddleupgallery.com

Printed and distributed by Marless Fellows

Library of Congress Publication Data

Fellows, Marless
   A Handshake is Enough / Marless Fellows and Leslie V. Bay

ISBN 978-0-692-02580-2
Library of Congress Control Number: 2014911084

Artwork photographed by CloudWatchers, LLC

First printing, 2014
Printed in USA

MIX
Paper from
responsible sources
FSC® C103525
FSC
www.fsc.org

TABLE OF CONTENTS

DEDICATION   5

MARLESS FELLOWS' STORY   7

     A Cowgirl Comes to Life

     A Cowboy's Wife

     This Cowboy Comes First

     Building A Career

     The Art Show That Changed My Life

     Opening Saddle Up Gallery In Cave Creek, Arizona

     Faces of The West

ARTWORK AND POETRY   26

INTRODUCTION TO THE POETS   101

POET BIOGRAPHIES   102

"How far you go in life depends on your being tender with the young, compassionate with the aged, sympathetic with the striving and tolerant of the weak and strong. Because someday in your life you will have been all of these."

— George Washington Carver

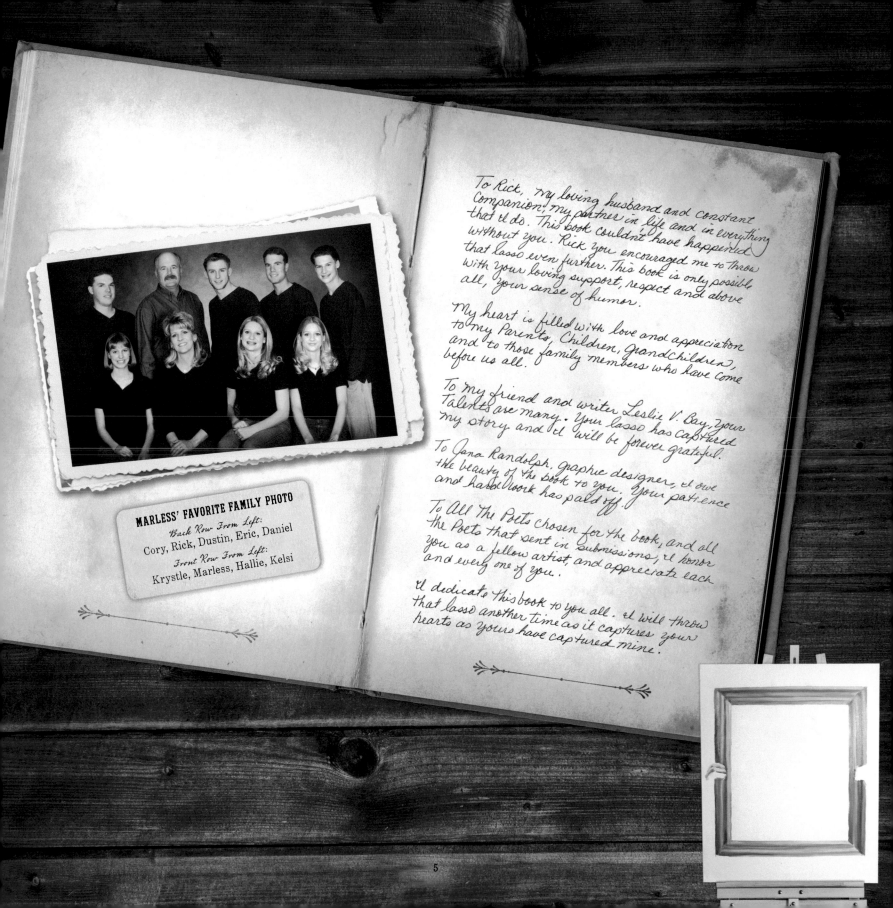

MARLESS' FAVORITE FAMILY PHOTO
Back Row From Left:
Cory, Rick, Dustin, Eric, Daniel
Front Row From Left:
Krystle, Marless, Hallie, Kelsi

To Rick, my loving husband and constant companion; my partner in life and in everything that I do. This book couldn't have happened without you. Rick you encouraged me to throw that lasso even further. This book is only possible with your loving support, respect and above all, your sense of humor.

My heart is filled with love and appreciation to my Parents, Children, Grandchildren, and to those family members who have come before us all.

To my friend and writer Leslie V. Bay. Your talents are many. Your lasso has captured my story and it will be forever grateful.

To Jana Randolph, graphic designer, I owe the beauty of the book to you. Your patience and hard work has paid off.

To All The Poets chosen for the book, and all the Poets that sent in submissions, I honor you as a fellow artist, and appreciate each and every one of you.

I dedicate this book to you all. I will throw that lasso another time as it captures your hearts as yours have captured mine.

NEW PASTURE

MARLESS FELLOWS

Written by Leslie V. Bay

There's a common thread that runs through my life, one that seems to have started generations ago with my Grandfather. That very thread turned into a cowboy's lasso, roping my Grandfather into WWI as a true American Cowboy in the US Cavalry. Breaking wild horses from Arizona to New Mexico, my Grandfather was a cowboy hero, "bronc busting" so that our soldiers would have a trusty steed to serve them well, freeing the world to independence. That lasso will live forever as my constant reminder as it is tossed and turned, hurling through the air, first circling my Grandfather then my Father and now me in so many different ways. It has captured us, bringing us back into its tightly spiraled grips – back to the love of the Southwest, the wild horses and the Cowboy Way of Life.

We are all intertwined as a family and impacted with so many different traditions by the Cowboy Way. It's the lifestyle that intrigues me and has wrapped me up like the warmth of an old Navajo blanket from the time I was a child. My family's lasso circles and circles above me, like the hawk soaring on drafts of wind that holds it up high above the desert on a day with a clear blue sky. The lasso captures me, so that I can share my love of the American Southwest, my intense love of horses, and the images that will preserve the rugged life of the American Cowboy through my art.

My goal is to portray what life was like as that American Cowboy of yesterday. A lifestyle of days gone by that can't be preserved as it was, yet one that I can share, symbolized through my art, and that of the poetry contained in this book. Paintings and poetry heighten the impact of each other. For me, it also allows me to understand that same life through the written word. My aim is to intertwine the two, sharing the strength of the cowboy soul and lifestyle through my art, and that of the cowboy poets' interpretation.

In today's life the cowboy has his smartphone, big trucks and ways of tracking the herd that they didn't have way back then – they just had each other to lean on – food, clothing, shelter and family kept the cowboy of the past moving. I like to believe that

"My Grandmother had the great strength of an old Ironwood tree on the outside, and a sense of humor that permeated the air like the sweet smell of orange blossoms that we all loved. What a character, known in town as "Granny."

– Marless Fellows

The
LASSO

Every good cowboy has his or her own style of Lasso. You never know whether you are going to have to rope in a bull or a bully!

The Lasso is a necessary piece of equipment made of rope that is strong enough to restrain a cow, catch a thief or just help you lead a horse to water.

Every rope has its own feel for the cowboy, and can actually be designed for the right or left hand throw. The weight is important for handling, too. The one end that forms the big loop to wrap around the neck of a cow or cinch its legs, is called a "honda," derived from the honda knot. It is usually reinforced with rawhide for ease of throwing and release.

Once the cowboy has his target captured, they can then use the horn of the saddle as an anchor and between the team of the horse and cowboy, you have one powerful tow truck!

—❦—★—❦—

those ethics and strength of character are still there today. Defending and caring for the inner soul of the West is what I do best with my lasso, which has turned into oils and paintbrushes so that I can capture a way of life to be written and painted into history, which comes in so many ways.

To hold a paintbrush, for me, is as though I am holding the hand of someone I love. Every movement splashes the color of life across the canvas, taking you on a western journey. It's like galloping across the desert. A rush of adrenalin surges as my mind's eye fills with ideas and drifts with the courage that dares me to fly. The life of the cowboy is changing, but you can show the past, present and future through the vibrant colors that I use in every painting I create.

The quintessential American Cowboy is a risk taker by nature. Every day can offer a new challenge. It's those challenges that I feel in every brush stroke, from the tough hide of a cowboy or cowgirl spreading their roots across the American Southwest terrain, just as I have done with my own family.

My Grandfather and my Father would regale me with their stories of the Old West. It taught me that the Cowboy Way was one of strength, muscle, vigor and endurance, mixed with honor, integrity, humor, a good story, and a love for the wide-open spaces. Never far was their trusted friend – their horse. Bringing those stories to the canvas will safeguard and defend the history of the working cowboy, giving you a glimpse of the past and one of the present. I look into the eyes of the rugged, weathered, leathery faces of the modern-day cowboys that I paint, the stories that those faces carry with them, and I know my Father and Grandfather would approve.

My Grandfather was born in 1895 in Childress, Texas, home of the true working American Cowboy. It's hard to believe he was drafted into the Cavalry at age 22, on June 5, 1917. Occupation listed on his draft card: Cowboy, place of employment: Matador Land and Cattle Company, with a history all its own. At times, I feel myself getting lost in dreams of the era and what he was feeling at such a point in history. The visions dance in my mind and that's how a painting is born.

He was getting up there in age and not yet married, but duty called and he was a cowboy through and through. Back then, the wild horses were plentiful in Arizona and New Mexico and the Army was in need. They engaged my Grandfather to capture the wild horses, and break those broncs so that they could be used as work horses. The horses were employed mainly for transporting the wounded and pulling artillery wagons. One's life is impacted for generations in ways you never thought possible. It's more than the six degrees of separation you hear about, it's that lasso that is still capturing my life and that of my family.

By now the war had ended and my Grandfather was still working to catch wild horses and selling them to ranchers in Carrizozo, New Mexico. Working with the chuck wagon behind him, and all of the cowhands together, I have the very photo of the scene that was taken by a traveling photographer to capture the essence of the West. All the cowboys were given clean white shirts that day so they could be photographed for the tourist postcards. The photo of my Grandfather is now depicted in one of my well-known paintings. The photo itself was transformed into a postcard way back then and sold to tourists passing through the Old West towns – already history in the making.

Even though Granddad was not a young cowboy he managed to catch a little filly – my Grandmother. At age 34, and at the time of the Great Depression in 1929, he married my Grandmother who was much younger. Poorer than a church mouse, they braved the Southwest making ends meet by moving from ranch to ranch, finding work where they could.

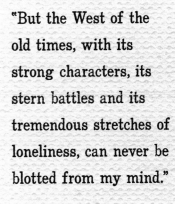

My Grandmother had the great strength of an old Ironwood tree on the outside, and a sense of humor that permeated the air like the sweet smell of orange blossoms that we all loved. What a character, known in town as "Granny." This will give a better idea of who she was and how she looked. Granny's two center fingers on her left hand were fused together, a look she didn't want to change. Leave it to Granny, she wore big "pinky rings" on both hands, long nails – how she did this as a rancher's wife with eight kids, God only knows.

My Grandfather was a gentle soul, even with all the bronc busting and tough life he was as kind as they come. Granny was fun loving but let me tell ya Granny was a strong woman and a true woman of the West. This woman had a huge sense of humor and loved to make everyone laugh with pranks and fun. In today's world she would have been a businesswoman. Back then, she was the CEO of the family. My Mom and her older sister were given the responsibility of helping to raise their siblings.

Out of my Grandparents' union came eight children, one of which was my Mom the second of eight. Born in 1931 in Carrizozo, New Mexico during tough economic times, Jonnie Jo Awbrey – can't get more western than that – was a bona fide western woman all the way. By the time my Mother was around nine, Granddad was running a pool hall to make ends meet. But like any good cowhand it was time to move on and take the family somewhere to find work. The whole family packed up, the whole family would work – they were Arizona bound!

"But the West of the old times, with its strong characters, its stern battles and its tremendous stretches of loneliness, can never be blotted from my mind."

– Buffalo Bill Cody

The
COWBOY
SPURS

There's nothing like the sound of a spur as it rattles down the trail. That distinctive sound as though two tiny symbols clang together. Those sounds come from what is called a "rowl," that spinning metal disk on the back of the boot heel. Star like points that spin around, ready to heed the message from rider to horse to "get a move on."

Wearing a spur is as everyday as puttin' on your belt. Hoist that boot up on the edge of a bench, buckle that spur around the heel, and you are ready to go.

The spur was an integral part of equipment in the Cavalry, attached to the regulation boots that each soldier wore. No doubt, Granddad (Roy Clarence Awbrey), wore these in his days of breaking horses for the Cavalry.

As my Mom tells it, "You've heard of cotton pickin' time? Well that's just what all us kids had to do. We did what we could, which meant we all picked cotton until Daddy found a ranch job south of Eloy, Arizona where he could use his cowboy skills. It was a cattle ranch and that was his thing. We all lived on the old ranch while Daddy took care of the cattle, branding and whatever it took to keep the ranch running. Keep in mind there were no bathrooms on the ranch just outdoor toilets, no electricity."

The school the Awbrey gang went to in those days was a one-room schoolhouse in the area known as "Green Reservoir." Somehow my Mom and her sister ended up in the same grade, a mix-up between New Mexico and Arizona. It didn't seem to matter to the girls, they held an eighth grade graduation party just for the two sisters, and all was good in the world.

About the time Mom went to high school, the family headed to Casa Grande, Arizona, where my Grandparents had opened up a *"help-yourself laundry."* Life on the ranch was getting difficult for an old cowboy to manage.

Mom had finally grown up and was a young working girl. She met a good-looking young cowboy, but that cowboy was headed off to the Navy. He was cute and could turn a girl's head, but not much of a thought was given and she moved on with her life. By now Mom was working in the local café in Picacho, Arizona. My Mom, Jonnie Jo, loves to tell the story, "I looked up one day and there he was right in front of me at the old café. Your Dad looked at me and said 'You're not married yet? Everyone else is!' I was 19 and you know I was very interested. Two weeks later we were married. In my day, that's what you did."

Dad was a cowboy from the ground he stood on to the crown of his cowboy hat, born in Oklahoma and coming to Arizona at age six. Dad had one brother and one sister, and a Mother who was the strong businesswoman, known for her flower shop. That's where I must get my business sense. His Dad worked odd jobs but they were dyed-in-the-wool cowboys.

His entire life Dad had been around ranches, but duty called at such a young age and he headed off for the Navy, stationed on an aircraft carrier. Not exactly what a cowboy would do, trade in his spurs for a ship, but it was wartime and he was needed. After his three-year stint in the Navy he had signed on for another six years just before my parents met. Daddy's history would include the Korean War and three tours in Vietnam – now *there* is an American story.

So Mom married the cowboy-turned-sailor and became Jonnie Jo Buchanan. The romance was fast and so was the marriage, my Dad headed off to San Francisco to board the ship. It was time to send for his new wife. Mom had never been out of Arizona since moving there as a child, but he told her to get on a train bound for the Golden Gates. Now if that isn't a woman of the West I don't know who is; brave as can be, off she went. For two months they lived in San Francisco before he left for overseas. Mom was pregnant with my oldest sister Jacque and didn't know it when Daddy left. Her pioneering strength got her through the hard times.

Here's a bit of interesting family lore; while my Mom was pregnant with my oldest sister, her Mother, my Grandmother, was pregnant with my Mom's youngest brother at the same time – yep that's the life of the cowboy and cowgirl!

As a child, by the time I came around, we were still traveling back and forth from California to Arizona because that was truly home. We would head to the docks to meet up with my Dad as his ship would power into port. After being in the Navy for 21 years and three tours of Vietnam, it was time for our family to settle back in Arizona. During his time in the Navy, my parents had purchased a little plot of land, about five acres in Apache Junction, Arizona. I was eight and glad to be settled into our little ranch.

As I look back, it was my Grandfather, Father and Mother, who each imparted some aspect of cowboy life to me. That depth of feeling, the work ethic, the rough and tough life of survival, and the intensity and profound character that was required by cowboys or cowgirls of their time, was inherited by me. That is how my paintings evolve, through that imagery of my life. The respect of the West hit each of us in some way or another. I think for me, my Father and I had a special bond that lived on and inspired me with our shared love of horses and the treasured feeling of that secret soul that is so deeply rooted in the cowboy.

A COWGIRL COMES TO LIFE

As long as I can remember the feeling of the Southwest ran through my soul. My horse, Sam, took me over some of the most spectacular terrain this country has to offer. Now I am able to paint the dreams and visions that waft around my mind like the campfire smoke that dances out of the flames. That's what I share with you.

"His entire life Dad had been around ranches, but duty called at such a young age and he headed off for the Navy, stationed on an aircraft carrier. Not exactly what a cowboy would do, trade in his spurs for a ship, but it was wartime and he was needed."

– Marless Fellows

John Andrew Buchanan, Korean War and three tours of Vietnam. Marless Fellows' Father.

I was born in Memphis, Tennessee – one of the many locations we were stationed while Daddy was in the Navy. We jumped place-to-place and dock-to-dock waiting for Daddy to return. By now there were a total of five in the family; I have two older sisters, Jacque and Carol, and somehow we all carry the gene of being artistic from both parents.

There is so much to be said about planting roots where you live, but the roots of my life didn't begin to flourish until they hit the hot, dusty, sun-scorched soil of Arizona. At such a young age I blossomed like the bloom on the great Saguaro, when we finally took root in the desert. It is here in Arizona that the cowgirl in me and the cowboy in my Dad found a permanent home on the Southwestern range along with my Mother and two sisters.

I should have guessed that the wild mustang churning inside of me, just waiting to race the open range was hereditary, passed down for generations, cowboy to cowgirl. It was time to carry on the traditions of the hardworking, soul-searching, fun-loving cowboy. The roots that first were planted by my Grandfather were spreading farther than he ever would have imagined.

Most girls just had wild imaginations, playing at being a cowgirl. We would get all dressed up with a gingham shirt, pearl snaps down the front, and a cowgirl hat. The hat, probably red, was dangling down our backs from a lariat tied around our neck. The boots would clop along the ground as we road circles on our stick pony, stories dancing in our heads of the Wild West. To most it was make believe. To me, this was the seed of a dream that grew into living the hard life of the West with all its extremes and all of its glories and adventures.

Daddy had bought property in Apache Junction, five acres – it was a job for him and served as a place for others to board their horses. It allowed him to introduce us to the cowboy way of life. Secretly, Daddy was yearning for horses as well, reaching back to his childhood in Oklahoma. From head-to-toe Daddy was a cowboy. He dressed like a cowboy, looked like a cowboy and lived the cowboy code: brave, fearless, honest, helpful, hard working and he loved his country. In fact, his nickname – you guessed it, Buck.

Even though times were tough for the family, the boarding of horses helped us all. It allowed the family to thrive both financially and emotionally. Daddy wanted to get horses so his daughters would start to take responsibility for animals. I credit my Father for raising all three girls in such a rugged lifestyle. My Mother, too, added to that western way of life, showing us the tough side of survival in the Wild West mixed with her soft inner nature too. That woman could sew up a storm and we were never without a prom dress!

Most people think of the men when they think of the life of a cowboy, but the women had to be stronger than you can imagine. Without the fortitude and backbone of the women of the West, the cowboy would never have survived the grueling nature of the work.

And so it began, all three of us little ladies would have to raise a calf from the beginning – this would teach us so much about a cowgirl's life. The first playful animal we all shared and cared for was our donkey – named Gypsy Rose. Good old Gypsy Rose, we could stand on her, you name it – she let us do it.

The next family member was a Shetland Pony named "Little Pete" – I just lived on him. Pete was amazing and best of all, my sisters were jealous because they didn't have a horse. In order to get back at me, they would give Gypsy Rose a kick in the shanks because they knew whoever was in front of her was going to get it – and so it was, she always bit me! Later, my Dad bought them horses, too, so that fun came to an end.

I lived on Little Pete, the best pony around and all my friends knew it was so. All of us kids were real buckaroos and there was nothing better than our horses. What an adventurous life we lived with such freedom. It was a tradition to saddle up our faithful pals, get our families together with their horses for a spectacular night ride. We would ride the night away 'til after midnight under the moonlight. I just can't remember a better feeling than that.

My Dad made an amazing cart for Gypsy Rose, so that my friends and sisters could load up and she would pull the cart with everyone piled on. We would go all over – I would be riding Little Pete, the Shetland Pony and if I was tired of riding on Pete, I would jump in the cart with all my friends and Little Pete would follow along. It was an amazing time to have such freedom in the Wild West.

We worked hard and took great care of all our animals. My Dad taught us how to care for them properly and he was the strict one – Mom was the doting sweet Mother we all needed. Because Daddy was strict, he expected us to do it all – we weren't pampered little girls by any means. We were the assistants as he changed tires, fixed cars, and we cared for our horses and cleaned corrals. That was the deal, we learned to clean hooves and brush down the horses. I never owned a bike – I would ride to my friend's houses – it seemed so natural, everyone had a horse and there was always a tree or post used for hitching.

Since we all rode, my friends were getting involved in small local rodeos called "Gymkhanas." I was around 12 when it was suggested to my parents that I get involved, too. Seeing as how I have quite the competitive streak, it was a natural thing for me to do, and seemed like it would be a heck of a good time. The one drawback for me was

"You know horses are smarter than people. You never heard of a horse going broke betting on people."

– Will Rogers

The
POSSIBILITIES BAG

In the Old West, they learned quickly that the possibilities were endless. There was the gold rush of course, and the necessity to have a place to stash your coins.

The Possibility Bag was a deerskin bag, fringed with a strap to sling over a shoulder, or wrap around the horn of the saddle.

The bag held some of the cowboy's cherished items, from trinkets like a pocketknife to flint for fires.

Pockets were few, as mountain men would find out, and the creation of the Possibility Bag grew to interest the cowboy.

Carry a bag, only you know what is inside, and what "Possibilities" lie ahead in your future.

that we didn't have much money, which meant no horse trailer. It wasn't going to stop me, that's for sure. It meant that I could only attend local "Gymkhanas" that were in riding distance, within five miles away.

Since Little Pete was too small, I needed a real horse for the competitions. My dad didn't waste any time looking, either. It turns out, that someone Dad was doing work for at the time had a horse that had been burned by fly insecticide. They had put the insecticide on her nose and all the hair was missing. Poor thing had been burned and scarred, but Daddy recognized a good horse and felt sorry for her. She came home with him one day, and from that day on we were inseparable. She was just right for me and I named her Sam. I had a competitive spirit and so did Sam – we were a perfect match! I started training and trained Sam too. I know now, that it was that competitive spirit in me that has driven me later in life to pursue the dream of being an artist, and that lasso just keeps reeling me in deeper and deeper.

Everyone pitched in to help out, the neighbors too, so that we all could get into the Gymkhana spirit. The neighbors helped, but then it was up to Sam and me. Daddy fixed up an area on the property and set up the barrels. Sam and I practiced so much that she was on autopilot, one little tap and off she went as fast as she could. There's nothing like riding a horse at a full run – what freedom! The crash of a barrel, cutting so close I could feel the whoosh of the metal, the pounding of the hooves, dirt flying and racing at the speed of light on my buddy Sam, gave me the cowgirl spirit for life. It is as indelible as the oils on my canvas.

No matter how much we trained, Sam and I always came in second or third, but it didn't matter because we were such close friends, we just kept trying. By now, boys were in the picture and there is nothing like a cowboy to turn a girl's head. Seems like Sam and I were going to have to slow down and let one of them catch us!

A COWBOY'S WIFE

"You can't keep trouble from visitin' but you don't have to offer it a chair!"[1]

Who knew that leaving home, on the only ranch I had ever known and moving to a new ranch would be as it must have been for my Grandmother and Mother all those years ago. Marrying your sweetheart right out of high school at age 18 was a real eye-opener and probably something that all the rodeos in the world hadn't prepared me for at all. As it turns out, your high school sweetie may not necessarily be your forever-love. I am happy to say that I do have that forever-love with Rick Fellows. My journey as a ranch

[1] *Don't Squat With Yer Spurs on, A Cowboys Guide to Life by Texas Bix Bender*

wife took me a long distance down many trails until I reached the proverbial "fork in the road." Sixteen years later, it would lead me to my painting career. I'll get into the career in a bit, but let me tell you about my early days.

Vince Dobson and I had been married for 16 years, which added to the lasso history from his family to mine. A lot was learned. A lot was taught. A lot was shared. And a lot was lost. We had four incredible children together. The legacy of the Southwest family has been etched in the Arizona soil and continues with our grandchildren, making us both so proud.

Let me tell you a bit about my early married life. It just so happened that my high school sweetheart came from a large farming and ranching family, growing the essentials from corn to cotton, wheat to watermelons, and everything in between including sheep. The family I married into had a history, a legacy that is still talked about in Arizona and across the country. This is where my history begins and ends on the Dobson Trail.

It all started in the 1880s. A true ranching family, they drove sheep from the deserts in the winter up into the high country in the spring. The trail that was used was called the Heber-Reno Sheep Trail Driveway. That trail was established in 1916. There used to be as many as 12 bands of 2,000 sheep. The trail days are over for the Dobsons, but the legacy lives on, painting pictures of its own in the Arizona landscape. The Dobsons were the last ones to use the driveway.

The Dobson family has such a rich heritage – my children are a part of that legacy. The family educated me so much about remaining close. Even though I came from a wonderful family too, I think that their history and the family devotion that my mother-in-law instilled in all of us taught me so much. Vince's Mom, Eileen Dobson, was such an extraordinary matriarch of a woman. She kept everyone together and made sure the family herd stayed strong – that was her job.

The role of matriarch draws an undercurrent that lives in the families of the West, like the bales of tightly wound barbed wire ready to unfurl and be strung post-to-post on the ranch fence holding it together. Keeping in all the good, while keeping out all the trouble. It's that sheer strength and will that I want you to feel in every painting – they have to tell the story of the West then and now. That is what I want to reveal with vibrancy and brush stokes, expressing the story in my art.

"One of my fondest memories is sitting around the campfire during the day. The herders would cook us some of the most incredibly delicious meals I had ever eaten."

Along the Dobson Trail

— **Marless Fellows**

15

MISCHIEF

The COFFEE POT

Now if that coffee ain't as dark as the midnight sky, and as thick as molasses, well then it just won't do the job of keepin' you up for that morning's daybreak and workin' the range!

Coffee was always brewin' over the campfire. The chuck wagon cook, usually known as "Cookie," better have a good cup of coffee over that fire 24/7. After all, the "Cookie" was workin' those cast iron pots and pans while the cowboy was working the herd. After a brief night's sleep under the stars, those cowhands needed their brew.

The coffee itself was made with just the grounds poured into the pot, and brought to a boiling hot temperature for those cold mornings and evenings.

Now none of that sissy stuff for the cowboy, those grounds were boiling 'til that coffee was good and hot.

Every good cowboy knows there are going to be a few grounds in the bottom of the cup, but the sunrise is worth every sip.

⸺ ★ ⸺

I believe that it is my responsibility to pass on to my children and grandchildren, that exhibition of strength, the love of social gatherings, and bringing the family in together. I learned from Vince's Mom, that you bring in your traditions and hold them close. You devote everything to your family, even in the tough times. You spend every day cooking, cleaning, taking care of your family, and that's what you did. On a daily basis you were taking care of someone. Vince's Mom was a little tiny thing with a big heart.

We lived close to my in-laws, set up in a tiny 600-square-foot house to start – it was ours and that was how it all began. Rent was one hundred dollars per month to my in-laws, and we were off into the family ranching life. Although Vince was really a farmer, we would go occasionally to the Dobson Trail. Once a year the sheep would be moved to the White Mountains, getting them out of the heat. The drives were startling, hundreds upon hundreds of sheep, men and horses all with one goal – make it through weeks on the trail, enduring some of the roughest of times to make it to the summer grazing land.

At the camps we would meet up with the herders just for the day to see what was happening with the herd and for a long awaited yearly social gathering. The herders were mainly Basque shepherds. Preserving the history of their traditions, known as some of the best herders that ever lived, was being carried out in the great Southwest.

One of the fondest memories I have is sitting around the campfire during the day. The herders would cook us some of the most incredibly delicious meals I had ever eaten. Sitting around the fire, not much English was spoken but we all could communicate and learn from each other. There was always a stretch of long wire strung tree-to-tree with long shards of meat patiently waiting to become jerky. The spring sun did its job of curing and drying the meat by the warmth of the day. As they headed up to higher elevation, the dried meat would serve as a great way to stave off hunger, as you reached the pinnacle of the mountaintop where the sheep would graze for the summer.

The cowboys there were always deep in conversation about trouble with bears and predators of the sheep, something that would get after them causing great harm to man and animal. Some were lost to the elements and the perils of the desert, but you had to press on. The smell of the fire, the fresh mountain air and hearing their stories always amazed me. The herders and their dogs were so trained. They always had their Australian Shepherds, like no other dog around; they could move a whole herd. A single whistle, a nip at the hind shank kept everything moving smoothly. The work was hard and could try the patience of any good herder. It took a good month and a half to get the sheep to the White Mountains. Just imagine running into bears and all kinds of animals – they were always on guard for the sheep and themselves, it's not an easy life.

As time marched on, I found myself as a young wife not knowing what to do with myself. I had always had an interest in a career of modeling. During high school, I went to beauty school. Actually, even before high school, beauty was my thing. I talked my Mother into letting me get my hair done in Mexico on one of our family trips. Where else could I get the highest "beehive" that ever lived! It was so tall, that in order to get into the car to go home, I had to get my head in first with the hair and then the rest of me!

So after we married I worked on hair, but Vince wanted me home. After all, I was the proverbial rancher's wife. Half the time he wasn't there and I would be on the ranch all by myself. That wasn't going to do for me, so after about a year and a half I decided to go into modeling. Well, getting pregnant didn't help that career!

Living way out on the family ranch in Mesa, Arizona, our little bungalow began to get cramped. There was another house on Vince's older brother's ranch that had some land, so we decided to move to larger quarters. The house was in major need of re-modeling. I remember, in particular, when we were to move in, the house had to be fumigated since it was on the ranch and infested with all kinds of critters. From the fumigating my face was covered in strawberry welts from ear to ear, all from the fumes – on a ranch it's all in a day's work. You marched on and let it pass.

I often say that life has seasons. For me there was the first season; getting married and having kids. I was 23 when I had my first child – at this point Vince ranched and I became a Mom. We had four children so life was hectic to say the least. Our kids were three, four, five and eight. The second season I didn't see coming at all; divorce. These are the times you see what you are made of, and I had to carry on. I took my four kids and had to get a job. All was going well until I was asked to work nights. Things just became a little more difficult with four kids to raise at such young ages.

I had gone into a dark hole, a place I had never experienced before. So I had to make a decision on how we were going to raise our children. It came down to the fact that I just couldn't do it all on my own. Vince and I decided to split up the kids – he took the boys and I took the girls – it was the only way and a very difficult decision.

As time passed I decided to go to divorce recovery class. The class saved me in so many ways. It was there that I sat next to the man that I would marry – Rick Fellows. Both of us were trying to figure out life. Rick was a pilot for America West Airlines, now US Air. He also had children, two boys and a daughter. Rick and I combined our families and now we were nine! Seven kids – who would have thought that this is how divorce class would end – 24 years later, we now have 13 grandchildren.

Marless Fellows' COWBOY COFFEE

I like to make my coffee good and strong and with cold water to settle the grounds.

★ Bring your water to a boil over an open campfire or stovetop.

★ Pour about a cup of grounds right into the boiling water – no filter needed for the Wild West! Give it a quick stir.

★ Remove the pot from the fire and add in a cup of cold water or just grab a handful of snow if that's what's nearby to help the grounds settle.

★ Grab a cup, pour yourself some coffee, and you'll feel right at home on the range.

The
HORSESHOE NAIL

With the horseshoe came the horseshoe nail. The nail is used to secure the shoe in place by the blacksmith or farrier.

The nails come in various shapes and sizes depending on the shoe used on the horse.

The nails are driven into the wall of the hoof so that the shoes stay secure. Each nail is bent in, curving towards the outside so as not to hurt the horse. The nails end up on the outside of the hoof, where the farrier cuts off the sharp points. He then files the horseshoe nail, for a smooth surface on the hoof.

Not only can the horseshoe be lucky, you may just get lucky number "seven" nails in the shoe!

When Rick and I married it allowed me to move on. The desert had always fascinated me and I was up for learning as much as I could. I became a docent at the Desert Botanical Gardens. I wanted to be educated, challenged; learn about all the plants – it was fantastic.

Life was moving along and all was grand. My kids were in junior high and high school. I was always doing crafts with them and loved to entertain. There was one defining moment when my husband's Grandfather came to visit us. He was a wonderful artist who loved watercolors. One day as my interest was piqued talking to him about his art he said to me, "You should try it." Off to the store we went to get the supplies – it didn't take much to get me in the saddle. He showed me what to do and I was totally hooked. I knew immediately that I needed training – I wanted to do it right and get all the instruction I could.

I started going to Mesa Community College, taking just the basic drawing classes, and I do mean basics – they showed us how to sharpen our pencils! Traditional techniques. I knew right then that I loved drawing and texture. After the basics it was off to life drawing class. This is where you really learn all there is to know about the human anatomy. I thought at my age, what more could be learned! But let me tell you, you learn to look at life in a different way from shadows, to lines, to shapes, to colors. Semester after semester – six to be exact, I drew the human body. The human figure is the hardest thing to draw – when you can master that, you can draw just about everything.

Learning to draw the body sensitizes the eyes. It is making the eye see things that someone else doesn't see. Shadows can be so fulfilling in a painting, the slightest bit of shadow, seeing what is different about that shadow, and then learning to get it on canvas. That's what I call a good day on the ranch.

As I've said, I really think that life truly has its seasons. There is a season for raising your kids, a season for being responsible, a season in my case for divorce, and now there is the season to be what I want to be – that wild and crazy cowgirl, a woman of the West who loves and lives the cowgirl life, and loves her cowboy Rick.

THIS COWBOY COMES FIRST

There's an old saying on the ranch that a rancher will always put the herd first above all else, because that's where your livelihood is – take care of the herd and it will take care of you. Then comes the ranch, a roof overhead, food, clothing, and shelter. Lastly, your family – that warm hug at the end of a long day on the trail. I am here to tell ya… this is one cowgirl who puts her cowboy first! It's that romantic perfect fit, like when you put on your favorite boots, then grab your trusted horse, and head on out on the range. It's all about the team to keep you safe.

Being from Montana, working the family ranch makes Rick a cowboy in every respect. He's definitely my cowboy – that lasso has room for two and then some. Rick was a cowboy of the skies I like to say, as a pilot for US Airways and prior to that with the US Air Force, for a total of 38 years. So his herding abilities in the sky, as well as raising seven kids, make him a champion of circling the herd. When you finally find the one you love, everything is possible – including a new career.

BUILDING A CAREER

After my community classes had taken me as far as possible, I realized where I needed to go in order to learn how to paint. I continued my education at the Scottsdale Artists' School where I took classes on color, which I am still learning and will forever more. There can't be enough classes to teach you about color. That's what makes painting so incredible, the slightest drop of color can impact your painting. I always explain to people that I am a colorist, filling the canvas with vibrant colors of the West, the kind that remind you of an Arizona sunset at the end of a glorious day in the desert.

I took several intense workshops a year, learning as much as I could from different renowned masters. I painted everything – live models, "two-leggers and four-leggers," people to horses, learning all there is about figurative art from the masters of today, with style that was exquisite.

You don't really know what it is that you love – you paint everything from cactus to mountains to still life. Once you find the thing that grabs you spiritually and emotionally it evolves, and you are drawn in, taken into its world and you evolve with it naturally. My world as you know, was the Cowboy Way of Life. I had never really repressed it, but it had been put on the back burner. Now that burner was a glow like the campfire at night. The embers were fueling my desire to show the world who I was and how I see that world today. All my memories came flooding back and I just had to paint.

One of the master painters I was learning from was Bruce Greene. A Cowboy Artist of America, there isn't one painting of Bruce's that doesn't tell the story of life. Bruce taught me that, and I was able to pull things from my life that were rich with the soul of a cowboy. A career was born.

"For the want of a nail
the shoe was lost,
For the want of a shoe
the horse was lost,
For the want of a horse
the rider was lost,
For the want of a rider
the battle was lost,
For the want of a battle
the kingdom was lost,
And all for the want of
a horseshoe-nail."

– Benjamin Franklin

The COWBOY'S HAT

The true icon of the American Southwest, the Cowboy Hat, made to fit just right and sit so proudly on the head. If that old cowboy were lucky enough, John B. Stetson may have made the hat.

Take a look at a cowboy's hat and the story of a rugged lifestyle unfolds. The daily wear and tear of the cowboy's world, carried within that hat.

That hat could do it all: keep the sun off your face, shoo away the flies and a perfect tool to scoop up water for you and your horse if need be.

From the cattle drive, where a bull may have trampled the hat, to that special hat he may have worn the night he took his girl dancing – every mark carries a story of yesterday and the triumphs of tomorrow.

❦ ★ ❦

I started painting horses, and things began to unfold. It's like the rising of the sun over the desert when you are just sitting there quietly atop your horse – all the sites and sounds around you begin to come alive. That's the feeling I get when I hold the paintbrush in my hand and the bright colors of the world around me feel like the rays of the sun hitting my face.

Everything began to progress in my career. One thing I haven't had the chance to do yet, which is on my "bucket list," is to attend an "Artist's Ride." You are taken out in a gathering spot where they have real Western actors all dressed in their western regalia, from cowboys and cowgirls to Native Americans reenacting a time period. This is strictly a photo session for the artist – you shoot that camera every which way you can, capturing the moment. It's the ride of a lifetime.

With every painting I create, I am growing as an artist. Style is a constant change for me. You loosen sometimes and other times you feel tighter. It's all about the vibrancy of the color. I want that warmth you feel when you gaze across the desert in the early morning sunrise, and the spiny tips of the prickly pear cactus look like they are aglow bathed in yellow. You can only portray that feeling with an understanding of color. Every painting for me has a different light and a different feel – I always learn something new about my technique and myself.

THE ART SHOW THAT CHANGED MY LIFE

By now you have to be asking yourself what was I going to do with all my paintings. Rick was asking too! With a bit of prodding from Rick, I decided to test the waters. Looking at your own works of art you begin to wonder – will anybody like these? Maybe I am just seeing them through my eyes.

I started off very slowly, heading to local farmer's markets and art walks. It's like the feeling of being out there, but afraid of your own shadow. The passion, the desire to enter in the world of art, and become a real player, pushed me to pursue greatness. I am constantly working to do things just a little better than before.

I have a really competitive spirit that started way back when I was a barrel racer. It is that spirit within me and the love of what I do, that propelled me on to greater shows. It's that passion within me that never leaves my soul, it gives me the courage to move on along the trail.

There are many shows that you can be involved in around the State of Arizona, but I had to choose the ones that fit my way of life. After working the circuit of art events for years, I finally decided that I would try to gain exposure in the Arizona Fine Art

Exposition. This is a juried fine arts event that combines all aspects of an artist's life. It gives you the feeling you achieve when you are actually in a gallery while still at a fine arts festival, one that is judged by peers, and allows the visitor to see the true inner workings of the artist's studio. Collectors come from around the globe looking for fine art; meeting over 100 artists in residence and having the ability to see the very piece they may purchase being created before their eyes. I adore the camaraderie of my fellow artists; after all, we are all in it together for three months in the winter under the "Big Top" tent. Just being together with other artists fills my soul.

As I began to grow and see that I had a future in art, I mustered up the courage to enter the Phippen Museum Western Art Show in Prescott, Arizona. This show is a highly juried art show with one important feature – as an artist of the West, you have the opportunity to be seen by the public and by other well-known Western artists.

On my first entrance into Phippen, two of the Cowboy Poets of Arizona just happened to be wandering around the show. They often peruse the art searching for someone who will be the chosen artist to represent the annual Arizona Poets Gathering that is held yearly in Prescott, Arizona. I had no idea that there even was a poets gathering in Arizona, so it came as quite a surprise. It was these two gentlemen that encouraged me to enter the 2010 Gathering with my work. I went home that night filled with ideas and began to research the event. There must be that one special piece that would represent my love and understanding of the West as well as my talents as an artist.

As it turns out, I was one of only two women artists to have ever been honored by the Arizona Cowboy Poets for their Gathering. The painting that was chosen was called "Mischief." It definitely represented the West – five hardworking cowboys gathered on bended knee, taking a breather from a long and dusty ride. Poet Slim McWilliams composed a poem called *Up To No Good* about the painting. For me, this was the moment that I knew there was a beautiful handshake between the painter and the poet. This was truly a great honor that I just can't describe to you except that it was the culmination of my life represented in art.

Now, in 2014, I have been chosen once again to represent the Cowboy Poets Gathering in Prescott, Arizona, with my work called "Cowboy Journal." Fitting wouldn't you say!

OPENING SADDLE UP GALLERY IN CAVE CREEK, ARIZONA

I had worked in a couple of galleries, one of which was a co-op where you could put in your time in exchange for having your art displayed. This started to get my juices going.

The
FENCING
BARBED
WIRE

Betcha' didn't know that a farmer from Illinois would be the man to help the American Cowboy tame the Wild West with the invention of barbed wire.

Well it's true. The final artful design, one that was tried by many to keep cattle in their place, was awarded to Joseph Glidden[2] in 1874 with a patent.

The wire spread quickly across the open plains and the Wild West, so that open grazing could be controlled. You didn't want to lose your herd, your prized possession, and the one thing that helped support your livelihood.

To this day, range rights and the protection of property play an important role in the life of the cowboy.

[2] Joseph F. Glidden Homestead and Historical Center www.Gliddenhomestead.org

I progressed to a wonderful gallery called Open Range Gallery. I loved working there. This gave me the opportunity to talk to people from all over the world and explain the story behind the works of art. As the old cowboys would say, "I had the burr under my saddle" to get my own gallery started.

I was showing my work in the Arizona Fine Art Expo in 2012. The owner of a small shopping strip approached me one day. They were interested in my art, and wanted me to open a gallery in their center. It didn't take long to perk up my ears, because the desire was already at work. I decided to go over and have a look. The center wasn't far from the Expo and it was in a town that is the epitome of the Old West – Cave Creek, Arizona. In fact, it is home to many working ranches and cowboys – what more could an artist of the West ask for in a location.

Let me give you a glimpse into Cave Creek. The town has withstood the march of time through the diligence of everyone who lives there. The heart and soul of the town is the cowboy and the Old West. From the moment you enter town, you feel your shoulders relax as the mountains rise above directly in your view. Traveling down the main street is like entering the O.K. Corral. Old West buildings, hanging wood signs, hitching posts set out front of stores for ease of tie-up for your horse. I swear if you were to close your eyes, Miss Kitty and the Marshall would be walking down the sidewalk greeting the guests.

Don't let the old-world feel fool you; there are some of the finest galleries, restaurants and shops all along the route. There it was, a beautiful western center in the heart of Cave Creek called Las Tiendas. I could feel my heart begin to race as I made that right turn and drove into the center. There is a well-known barbecue restaurant at one end; wafts of smoke perfumed the air. Right in the center as you turn in was the shop that would become Saddle Up Gallery. I could tell from the moment I saw the space and talked to the other owners, this would become the home to my art. It was a place that just beckoned me to come in, set up shop, and start the rest of my life.

Rick had retired as a pilot, so we packed up our home of 23 years and decided to sell so that we could move to Cave Creek. We found ourselves getting to know the town's people and getting into the western way of life, the life we had both come to know so well.

There was not much work to be done, some painting of the gallery walls to make it complement the works of art I would be showing, but the bones of the structure were right there, just waiting for the sign to be hung.

FACES OF THE WEST

Since opening Saddle Up Gallery and getting to know the locals, I had an idea one day that I would like to paint the cowboys and cowgirls in town. There were so many of them that stopped by to see my work, it seemed only natural to spread the word about my idea. I decided to paint 28 portraits each with a story to tell, and it would culminate in a gathering of locals called "Faces of the West." Spreading like wildfire in no time the word went out. Before long I had 28 of the most fantastic faces and stories that showed the West was alive and well, living in Arizona.

Keep in mind, I was entering my sixth season with the Arizona Fine Art Expo. The Expo started in January and so did my call for cowboys and cowgirls. I had a one-hour sitting to begin the painting and photograph them so I could finish their portrait. I would complete all 28 prior to March 16th, 2013. Not a bad start for a new gallery owner. Nothing like a little bit of pressure to get to know the town-folk! They streamed in as word got out. I would paint their portrait and for the sitting and allowing me to tell their story, they were gifted their original painting.

The night of the unveiling was amazing. Hundreds of people showed up to hear some good old cowboy ballads sung by Gail Starr, sip a little wine, and just gather and talk about what was happening on the ranches. Everyone enjoyed the portraits and reading the stories of each and every participant. It turned out to be a night to remember. To this day, I have no idea how I was able to get it all finished in time.

Now you see how I grew up, and how I *continue* to grow with my love of the West continually pushing me forward. Saddle Up Gallery is off and running, and my purpose in life is being fulfilled. I'm "Lassoing the West in Art," one painting at a time, where the cowboys say *A Handshake is Enough*.

"Keep your eyes on
the stars, your feet
on the ground."

– Theodore Roosevelt

RUSTY

WAITIN'

Written By
Sam DeLeeuw

He's lookin' forward to today.
It's gonna be their second date.
It's 5:00am, the sun's come up!
This cowboy really hates to wait.

Said she'd be there by 4:30!
Would meet him by his open gate.
"Musta stopped fer gas and coffee.
That's no excuse for bein' late!"

The first date went quite well, he thought.
They siphoned water to the stock.
She took the hose, inhaled real deep!
The backwash came as quite a shock!

Water went spewin' out her nose!
She dang near drown and choked to death!
He Heimliched once and then again!
Pumped 'til she fin'ly caught her breath!

Gettin' dark he explained to her
Old Rusty had lost each headlight.
Handin' her the glaring search lamp,
He shoved her on the hood in fright.

As she straddled the rusty hood,
She was to light the road ahead!
She was fine 'til he hit that hole!
She skidded through a cactus bed!

He told her he had some Band Aids
Fer her elbows, her knees and head.
Used his pliers to pluck the spines!
Her look filled him with instant dread!

Didn't know a lady like her
Would know words like she was usin'!
Smilin', he tossed her on the truck,
Findin' all this quite amusin'!!

Just stars and her to light the way,
It was a real romantic night.
How could she resist this rancher?
He figgered things were goin' right!

Well, he's still waitin' on that gal.
He's got great news when she appears.
She's ridin' in the back today!
Gets to pitch hay off to the steers!

They'll preg-check first calf heifers,
Then, there are calves to brand and cut.
She'll get to share the cab with him
And that slime caked heeler mutt.

She must have something wrong with her
Not wantin' to be together!
Life doesn't get better than this–
Cows, sweaty horses and leather!

One day the right gal will come by
Who'll love this ranchin' way of life.
She'll love his truck and love his dog,
And love being this cowboy's wife!

COMPANION

REDEEMED

Written By
Gary Penney

I guess I was just lucky
When I stumbled on to him.
They said he had no future
And his life was looking grim.

He'd throwed the little daughter
Of the man who run this spread.
Jake had no patience for him;
Said he'd like to see him dead.

Sheer luck brought us together
Before he was hauled away.
Jake told me I could have him
But, "Be out of here..... today".

I stepped in for this gelding
And saved him from his fate.
Some men don't think too clearly
When their minds are filled with hate.

A life can be worth saving
If you'll spend a little time.
My life got a second chance
When God gave His Son for mine.

I, too, was thought a loser
In the eyes of many men.
But I gave my life to Jesus
And He took away my sin.

Two misfits found each other
With no trouble, doubt, or fears.
A faithful friendship was begun
That has lasted through the years.

From the start I felt his love,
Like he'd pledged his life to me.
This horse was my reminder
Of what Jesus means to me.

Trust is gained from true respect
Where you feel the love both ways.
One won't let the other down
Through bright or darkened days.

Try to find the good in bad.
Make some time to stop and pray.
Help a horse or fellow man
And make a difference every day.

Since I've learned to trust in Him
I've never had a doubt.
God gave me a second chance
So I've tried to make it count.

A partnership formed by fate
We ride the range together.
Working cows or dodging thorns
Through sun or stormy weather.

Riding on the sun lit plains
Or through dark and endless canyons,
I trust in God and my horse
'Cause they're my true companions.

DADDY'S LITTLE GIRLS

HERITAGE

Written By

Phil Ellsworth

It often seems for GOOD,
To continue on its path,
It has to have a beginning.
One that will surely last.

What is cherished in this life,
Must be taught in many ways.
Through experience and example,
And lived throughout our days.

For the GOOD to last a lifetime,
It needs a strong foundation.
A beginning with memories,
That stir the imagination.

Sometimes it takes a hero,
That may just be a Dad,
That holds a faith inside,
To guide through good and bad.

The thing that makes it all worthwhile,
Is to see it carried on.
To watch the GOOD continue,
Through kin, a daughter or a son.

That's HERITAGE!

COWBOY'S PLAYGROUND

OUR OWN HERD

Written By
Greg Harwood

Ole Jim and I were out of work
No jobs were to be found
We were gettin' pretty desperate
There just wasn't much around

Now we've been through some tough times
And we've had a scrape or two
But our bellies were so empty
You could almost see right through

Then Jim had an idea
And he shared his thoughts with me
He laid it out so simple
It was plain for me to see

We'll gather up our own cow herd,
Jim suggested with a smirk
Though it will take a little time
And an awful lot of work

We'll go a huntin' maveriks
And gather up some strays
Brush poppin' is the kind of work
That we do anyways

We'll not rope any branded calves
We won't be called a thief
Those fellers using running irons
Are just asking for some grief

There's lots of cattle in the brush
Unbranded, wild, and mean
But that don't mean a thing to us
That's nothin' we ain't seen

Well I guess we'd best get started
So pull your cinch up tight
And snug your hat down on your head
Cause we're headed for a fight

Now shake out your reata
And build a loop that's wide
We'll rope a wild cow or steer
And brand his ornery hide

But this time we'll be burnin' on
A brand that's all our own
We'll be ropin' and a brandin'
Till a good size herd we've grown

Then we'll head 'em north for Kansas
Along the Chisolm Trail
We'll drive 'em towards Dodge City
At the slow pace of a snail

We'll graze 'em while we're trailin'
Hope they gain a pound or two
We'll make a lot of money
When this trail drive is through.

ANNIE'S GOT HER GUN

COWGIRLS ARE LADIES

Written By

Sam DeLeeuw

In the corral, she's just called "Gal",
She's as tough as any other.
Timid she's not with each calf caught,
"Y'all, git ropin' a nuther!"

Her face is wet from salty sweat,
Hands calloused, freckled and tan.
Chinks that are stained, a back that's pained,
She's partner and wife to her man.

She can talk gruff when work gets rough.
It just comes with workin' their stock.
At "hell or damn", it's "Scuse me, ma'am?"
As the boss's lady they mock.

By end of day, they've earned their pay.
Then as dirty cowhands will do,
Head to the trough, slosh green stuff off,
Not lettin' her close 'til they're through.

This grimy pack will soon be back!
It's her birthday party tonight!
Roasts on the spit, 'bove open pit.
Angus cuts are pinked up just right!

Guests at the gate at just past eight,
Bringing birthday gifts to their host.
Hand tooled saddle, chinks for cattle,
New six gun! The varmints are toast!

Just hours before, dirt, blood and gore
Splattered her from hat to her boots.
Wouldn't know now, she smelled like cow
The wrangler from their brandin' chutes!

Her smile is bright, oozes delight
At havin' close friends at their place.
She calls each name, so glad they came.
Contented smile upon her face.

She rides, she ropes, she dreams, she hopes.
A good choice she made for her life.
She's a fierce friend, a hard workin' hand,
First, a *lady*...then rancher's wife!

DOUBLE STARE

SO LONG, PARD

Written By

Ol' Jim Cathey

They stood in their traces, patient an' calm,
Ol' Ned an' Tobe at their best.
The Circuit Rider ended with a psalm,
as Papa Hop was laid to rest.

This pair of Morgans had come in a trade,
business was often done that way.
Papa was shrewd an' not easily swayed,
was pleased at the end of the day.

These Morgan horses were loyal an' smart,
would stay at task through it all.
They'd give their best, had plenty of heart,
workin' from early morn until nightfall.

Papa treated them with a gentle hand.
He expected them to do right.
He was firm, but quick to understand,
an' never put them in a tight.

He always made sure they got good care,
especially after their work.
He'd rub them dry an' let them roll somewhere,
this task he would never shirk.

The harness was always hung on its rack,
so it would properly dry.
Papa diligently took care of his tack,
he'd accept no alibi.

He made sure they got grain, if he had it.
Hard work shore 'nuff requires good feed.
An' the tack always snugged for proper fit,
why, this was just part of a horseman's creed.

They worked the fields pert near sun-up to sundown,
like Papa, they just did not tire.
Most Saturdays, they took us all to town,
with harness shined so folks could admire.

Sundays, Ol' Ned an' Tobe took us to preachin'.
Their rest would come when we got home.
For this, these ponies did not need teachin',
they'd find a shade an' never roam.

Those horses knew that Papa was their pard,
even when he was away.
So when Papa went to be with the Good Lord,
those ponies would be okay.

An' so, magnificent care would be theirs
while they spent their later years,
fer they were the answers to prayers
to these hardy pioneers.

They stood in their traces patient an' calm,
Ol' Ned an' Tobe at their best.
The Circuit Rider ended with a psalm,
as Papa Hop was laid to rest.

SHUTEYE

IN GOD'S HAND

Written By
Ol' Jim Cathey

His day had started at daybreak,
an' things jest got worse from there.
If it could go wrong, it shore did,
an' he was soon filled with despair.

You see, trials an' tribulations
shore tend to weigh a feller down.
He needs to get off to hisself,
jest to get rid of his dang frown!

A feller needs to sort things out,
so he sought a place way out yonder.
Johnny Mack had found this meadow
whar he could reflect an' ponder.

A hidden nook among the rocks
whar he could work things out.
Face his demons and darkest fears
an' clear his mind from all doubt.

He'd put his pony out to graze
an' put the coffee pot to warm.
With these chores done, he was ready
an' his ol' thoughts began to swarm.

He stretched out to gaze at the stars,
but this day had been a bit hard.
Snugged his hat down an' with a sigh
he drifted, 'cuz he was shore tired.

The late spring spell brought coolness,
an' he slept in the firelight's glow.
Surrounded with sounds of the night
an' his saddle for a pillow.

But then, his mind was tormented
with memories from a time past,
that eerily swept him along
as they berated an' harassed.

Bad memories full of darkness,
swirlin' an' engulfin' his soul.
Paralyzing him with a fright
as he spiraled out of control.

An' a chill seemed to surround him
as he lay on that prairie sod.
Then a thought seemed to remind him;
that he was protected by God!

When this promise came to his mind,
bringin' a light to the shadows.
His restless soul was put at ease;
caused his fears to decompose.

This sweet promise he had received
just as he thought he'd reached trail's end.
A promise that relieved his fears,
helped him find a heavenly friend.

Shore makes our life's path easier
when we come to understand
that troubles tend to melt away
when we place our cares in God's Hand.

YOUNG WRANGLERS

40

POINT THE WAGON TONGUE NORTH

Written By
Ol' Jim Cathey

The old Studebaker was parked
southeast of Double Mountain Peak.
That ol' wagon tongue pointed north,
markin' the direction we would seek.

It was near noon on that Sunday,
Ol' Cousy would soon ring the bell.
He'd scorched beef steak, biscuits, an' beans,
that cobbler shore had a good smell!

Boss claimed, "It was the day of rest."
So, Ol' Cousy read from the Book.
The fellers listened to what he read,
but they had a melancholy look.

They just lazed around that mornin'
while the herd rested an' grazed.
They'd swapped lies an' told stories
about how each one had been raised.

These boys was all a bit lonesome,
reminiscin' of days gone by.
Each of their thoughts seemed to settle
on sweet hearts an' Mom's apple pie.

Snort McCoy stood with propped up foot,
an' he told a shore 'nuff wild tale!
Ol' Sandy Joe just shook his head,
he claimed this story was mighty pale.

But, Jim Bob said it could've been so,
fer he had heard it said before.
While Freddie Scott sat with a frown,
an' said it pert near made him sore!

Them boys were shore gettin' restless.
Cousy had best hurry with the grub,
'cuz they needed to get hossback
an' stop this festerin' hubbub!

They'd gathered the Cayuga range,
where many wild Longhorns were found,
that hid in the rocks an' thick brush,
'til cowboys come pokin' around.

They'd slapped the quarter circle C
on many a mavericks hide.
Then headed 'em north to Abilene,
a mighty long an' dangerous ride.

They'd made good time comin' this way,
the weather had shore 'nuff been swell.
The Boss thought to rest them cattle,
then head 'em up the Chisholm Trail.

Ol' Jessie Chisholm forged that trail
from his trading post on the Red.
Many Texas herds came through here
before moving to Abilene's railhead.

Wal, them boys had eat an' rested.
Soon, back in their saddles they'd be,
where they'd circle them steers an' sing
softly… a soothing melody.

GOTCH YOUR BACK

GREENER GRASS

Written By

Greg Harwood

We calve in March when the weather's fair
And the temp ain't ten below
In a pasture by the river
There, protected from the snow

It's almost more than we can do
While feedin' bales of hay
And watchin' out for newborn calves
We're workin' night and day

Insufficient winter feed
Has been our greatest fear
But the cows are healthy, slick and fat
They've wintered good this year

We're a little short on help
We could use another hand
With a thousand head of mother cows
And a thousand calves to brand

We'll work from can see till we can't
Till all the Brandin's done
We'll vaccinate and castrate
No time for havin' fun

With summer round the corner
We'll quit feedin' bales of hay
The pasture's gettin' greener now
And brighter every day

And when we get the Brandin' done
The boys will all commence
To hammer staples, stretch some wire
And tighten up the fence

Winter weather makes a mess
Of fences built from wire
But with some work we'll have a fence
That we can all admire

And now that summertime is here
We've turned out the bulls
We've sorted out the dry cows
The old ones and the culls

We use the best bulls we can find
From breeders far and near
To wean the biggest calves around
Has been our goal each year

When buyin' bulls we do our best
To search their family tree
We spend some time a lookin' at
Their genealogy

We look close at their birth weight
And discuss their calving ease
Genetics are important
As well as EPDs

Each bull must pass a list of tests
To prove he's not a dud
Semen, Trich and PAP tests
To certify each stud

With mother cows raised here at home
Each writes an autograph
When crossed up with a purebred bull
They throw a fancy calf

And now that warmer weather's here
And wintertime is past
I'll go and open up the gate
And head for greener grass.

TRIFECTA

PARDS

Written By
Skylar Harwood

No words can express
How ya feel deep inside
Of the blessing God grants us
To cowboy and ride

There's no other job
Come the end of the day
Where your pride and your lifestyle
Mean more than your pay

There's jobs where they give ya
A nice car to drive
If bein' backed up in traffic
Makes you feel alive

But for folks like ourselves
That just ain't enough
Include laptops and cell phones
And all a' that stuff

We're spoiled, I know it
Though it's tough to see
But there's things more important
To you and to me

Like the privilege of sittin'
There high in your kak
Cinched to your old pard
Lettin' him have the slack

All the memories made
As your workin' your spread
"Lord, please let me cowboy,
Or let me be dead"

But of all the great blessings
That come with this life
Most important of course
Is my kids and my wife

Then I have other help
That I won't fail to mention
Who's only pay is some vittles
And the slightest attention

Just a scratch on the ear
Or a pat on the head
For my old dog and horse
And to keep em both fed

There's not a soul as ambitious
As Hank or Ol Blaze
Who'd be as dedicated
To work all their days

They've both earned my trust
And when things do get wild
They take care of me
As if I were a child

And for all that they do
I try and be fair
By keepin' em healthy
For this hard workin' pair

I keep Ol Blaze shod
And they both getta rest
Though the days are so long
But I'm doin' my best

We all work together
We have each other's back
Never draggin' our tails
Or not pullin' our slack

And they never complain
They just love what they do
So take care of your pards,
And they'll take care of you

MOVIN' THE HERD

FALL ROUNDUP

Written By
Greg Harwood

We saddle up at 5 AM
And ride out for the day
By the time we get this roundup done
We'll sure have earned our pay

The colts we ride are green broke
They're broncy and they're tough
The country sure is pretty
But it's raw and wild and rough

There's big high mountain meadows
With grass up to their knees
Tall quaking asps and pine trees
As pretty as you please

Rough and rocky mountain peaks
To make the scene complete
They stretch themselves toward the sky
And reach 12,000 feet

We're riding for the H+ Bar
Fall roundup time is here
Our neighbors come to help us
Some from far and some from near

600 head of cows and calves
Are moved to winter feed
We keep the herd a going
As the trail boss takes the lead

We follow through the oak brush
And past the old stock tank
I ride around behind the herd
Positioned on the flank

We whistle and we holler
Joe cracks his ole bull whip
The cow dogs bite 'em on the heels
And sometimes on the lip

We'll trail 'em off the mountain
It'll take a day or two
Then sort the calves for shipping
When the trail drive is through

The cows are slick and shiny
The calves are sassy fat
The grass was good this summer
And ya can't ask more than that.

THE MITCHELL

RIDIN' FOR THE BRAND

Written By
Greg Harwood

I stir at the fire and try to wake up
As I stare at my empty old coffee cup
I look at the sky the big dipper hangs low
One cup of coffee then it's my turn to go

It'll soon be my guard I'll ride out in a bit
But first I'd sure like a hot cup to sip
To rev up my motor and give it a start
To warm up my belly my hands and my heart

I ride the last guard it's the best time of night
The air fresh and clean and the stars shining bright
Like fires in the sky from camps long ago
They twinkle and shine with a comforting glow

I smell the coffee as it boils in the pot
And pour me a cup that's steaming and hot
Then enjoy the aroma that drifts past my face
Rekindling old memories that time can't erase

Of camps long ago of trail drives and cattle
Of long dusty trails as I sit in the saddle
With cow hands and Cookie and ornery old bosses
Wild cattle, rough country and broncy, rank hosses

After 35 years of trailing a cow
I guess it's the only job I know how
Early morning, last guard it's the best place for me
There's no where on earth that I'd rather be

My night horse is saddled, I'm ready to go
I just want to finish this hot cup of Joe
So here I sit with a cup in my hand
Content with my life cause I ride for the brand.

MISCHIEF

UP TO NO GOOD

Written By
Slim McWilliams

They were five salty cowboys,
With more than a little pride,
There weren't a critter they couldn't rope and tie,
Not a bronc they couldn't ride.

So when they come across that old she bear,
Just a strollin' up the slope,
They knew right off they'd have some fun,
And they all shook out their ropes.
Five cowboys, five ropes and five horses;
Up to no good.

Juan got the jump on the rest of them,
His sorrel horse sure could fly.
He roped a head and a foreleg,
And dallied as he rode by.

But as he turned off Juan remembered
What it was that he'd forgot;
His loose cinch let his saddle turn
And Juan knew he was in a spot.
Five cowboys, five ropes and five horses,
Up to no good.

Now Juan's saddle was turning plumb sidewise,
His reata burns through his hand.
Juan kicks free from his stirrups,
And lands – next to the bear – in the sand.

Sandy rode in to help Juan out,
His loop caught the bruin's neck neat.
Jake turned his paint horse in behind,
And he scooped up two hind feet.
Five cowboys, four ropes and four horses,
Up to no good.

Sandy set the air on his gray horse,
Givin' Juan a chance to hightail,
But Jake's paint ducked in behind Sandy,
And his rope sucked up under Gray's tail.

Well Sandy's gray horse come plumb untrained
With that rope up under his tail,
He bogged his head and planted Sandy,
Then he lit off down the trail.
Five cowboys, three ropes and three horses,
Up to no good.

Ned saw that the wreck was growin',
But he figured "Aw what the heck",
His roan came up fast on the bear's right side
And Ned's hoolihan circled its neck.

Ned's turnin' right, Jake's off to the left,
The bear's sure caught in between,
And Earl's tryin' to bend that big black colt,
That's stampedin' away from this scene.
Five cowboy, three ropes and three horses,
Up to no good.

Ned flips his rope up over his head,
And dallies before it comes tight,
Jake's dallied and sets his paint in the ground,
Looks like they'll stretch him out right.

But right then Earl returns to the scene,
That black's a coverin' the ground,
He runs into Jake's paint with a full head of steam,
And the whole thing starts comin' unwound.
Five cowboys, three ropes and three horses,
But it ain't goin' good.

Jake's paint horse goes down, his dallies come free,
The bear's headin' for Ned and his roan.
Earl's about out of sight and Ned knows when to quit,
He'll not take that sow on alone.

Ned turns loose of his rope, Earl comes circlin' back,
And five punchers now watch with a chill;
That bear's coilin' four ropes and drivin' two horses,
As she disappears over that hill.
Five cowboys, one rope and three horses,

Up to no good.

MOVIN' ANGUS

52

SMELL OF HORSE

Written By
Sam DeLeeuw

The smell of horse is best of course
In fall when he's sweaty and hot.
This colt you ride, that gives you pride,
Last spring, was the best of the lot.

Starting him slow, you let him grow
To the role of workin' cow horse.
Snorty at first, he bucked his worst,
He sunfished with muscle and force.

This job demands, "Be light of hands"
When takin' on a three year old.
Kindness will tell, patience as well,
If their mouths will be hard and cold.

No human hand had touched his band,
Any day since he was a foal.
Soft be your talk, quiet your walk,
Approachin' the colt of charcoal.

Now there is trust, which is a must
If a man and horse work as one.
There's no abuse t'ward this cayuse
Gentlin' him had been lots of fun.

He's grown this fall, fifteen hands tall,
He's balanced in muscle and stride
Showin' his cow, through stock he'll plow,
Ears pinned for one hell of a ride!

Touch of the heel, he knows the deal,
Two jumps ahead of the leaders.
He'll plant and spin, and go again
Cuttin' off the steers and breeders.

He's quick and sure, he's got the cure
For that itch ev'ry cowboy feels
Of livin' free and glad to be
Workin' horses for bunk and meals!

With ev'ry turn there's more to learn
But Blackie is more than willin'
He never tires, all he requires?
A pen full of cows, just millin'.

The smell of horse is best of course
In fall when he's sweaty and hot.
This colt you broke, that's black as smoke,
Today is the best of the lot!

SADDLE UP

CRASH COURSE

Written By
Daniel Dobson

You could say I was mad at first,
When my horse ran out of sight.
A cubby of quail had spooked him up
And I was no match for his might.
I grabbed the horn and tried to hold
The reins of the rearing beast,
But my cinch strap came loose,
So my saddle and I……...flew…until we ceased.

I laid in the dirt, catching my breath,
So angry at what had occurred.
I sat up and yelled at the cowardly horse,
But he was too far away to have heard
It was just then when my trusty dog Crash,
Who joins me on every ride,
Slowly approached, with his aging dog wobble,
And sat down right at my side.

He looked down at me, as if to say,
"Come on, let's saddle up!"
Something I had told him a million times
Since he was just a pup.
He realized quickly what I did not,
That a hard road lay in store,
And the quicker that I got up,
The quicker we'd get where we were aiming for.

I look back now and I couldn't say,
The name of the horse that I scorned,
And old Crash has long since past.
He's been buried and he's been mourned.
I'm so glad I can remember that day,
Not as one where I was mad.
But, of a day I spent with a good friend of mine,
The best walk we ever had.

SASSY

LUCILLE

Written By
Sam DeLeeuw

She's sassy and bold
Her hair is spun gold.
He's in love with the girl on the billboard.
She's sportin' fringed chinks.
She grins as she winks.
Into her brushed denim jeans she is poured!

To him she's quite real.
He's named her… Lucille!
Her name whispered like a reverent prayer.
He can't sleep at night.
His mind is not right.
It's become a full fledged *billboard affair*.

Her jacket that's fringed
Has got him unhinged.
Sweet Lucille has since numbed his defenses.
Those tight fittin' clothes
As she strikes a pose
Has caused this cowboy to lose his senses.

Each day to this miss
He throws her a kiss
As he passes in his automobile.
No gal in this life
Will be his sweet wife.
This heartsick cowboy's in love with… *Lucille!*

SHARED DREAMS

DREAM CATCHER

Written By
Ol' Jim Cathey

They perched upon that top rail, each one traveling their own trail.
The young lass and her loving Dad, with thoughts of the good times and bad.
She'd ask his thoughts, seek his praise and to the hills they both would gaze.

Most every day, they chose this place, a chance to ponder and seek God's grace
in stillness of the desert air, their thoughts and feelings to compare.
But, now they sat silently, it's hard for young and old to agree.

The old man's heart is heavy now, the future sure seems bleak, somehow.
His hopes for her dreams are growing dim, 'cuz her thoughts did not agree with him.
He thought he knew what was best to be, knowing that her Mom would sure agree.

He knew that she should go back East, for sure now, with her Mom deceased,
her education to complete, and maybe a young man for her to meet.
Yet, he also knew she had the grit, she had the heart, she'd never quit!

She quietly sat upon that fence, and pondered thoughts that were intense.
Her feelings stirred within her breast, she vowed she'd stay here in the West.
Her heart and eyes searched for destiny, while she basked in that naivety.

The early days when times were hard, life demanded constant guard,
a simple life had been their lot, yet, seems that way has come to naught!
Neighbors on the horizon loom, they're slowly losing elbow room.

And then her dreams strayed, beyond the hill, and sought the answer that would fulfill
a lifetime goal, which of course, seemed to include her love, the horse.
Their thoughts would take a certain turn, and one by one they'd soon discern,

for a time his dreams for her must wait, allow her dreams to liberate.
So they sat side by side and smiled, with grand thoughts running wild,
and both agreed to make this stand, they shared this love for life and land!

SOUNDS OF THE WEST

STICKER'S LULLABY

Written By
Gary Penney

As day turned into twilight
It came time to get some rest.
This day had been a long one
And each hand had done their best.

We'd gathered up the yearlings
On this land that we call home;
Marked 'em with our branding irons
Then we set 'em free to roam.

Old Dan had baked some dumplings
And a plate of beans for each,
Followed by a great dessert
Of sweet cobbler made with peach.

We lazed around the campfire
Feeling good about our day.
Sticker pulled his guitar out
And began to softly play.

The strings began to vibrate
As he sang his song of choice.
We'd heard him play his guitar
But we'd never heard his voice.

His voice was like an angel
As he sang his western song.
He played "Red River Valley"
And we began to sing along.

We sang about the "Tumbleweeds"
And the "Rose of San Antone".
We got "Back in the Saddle Again"
With an "Old Cowhand" we've known.

We sang about "Cool Water"
Like the Sons of the Pioneers.
Then "The Yellow Rose of Texas"
Almost brought us all to tears.

We rode "Along the Navajo Trail"
Which shouldn't seem so strange.
Just a bunch of buckaroos
Who love our "Home on the Range".

Sticker picked them one by one
As he played the songs we knew.
We sang songs from Gene and Roy
And Patsy Montana, too.

We sang about the cowboys
And the way of life out West.
Sticker picked out all he could
Till his fingers needed rest.

But now our fire was waning
And we knew our day was done.
We crawled into our bedrolls
As t'was time to end our fun.

Then, as we were turning in,
And we thought the songs were through,
Sticker bid us all goodnight
With a "Happy Trails" to you.

Sticker gave us all a peace
When he finished off our day.
Made us glad that we're all cowboys
And we live the Cowboy Way.

TEAMWORK

TALKIN' EYE TO EYE

Written By
Gary Penney

He raised me from a puppy,
The master I look up to.
He tried to teach me right from wrong;
What I should and shouldn't do.

It wasn't always easy,
'Cause I had a stubborn streak.
Thought I knew much more than him
Till I learned to hear him speak.

We started with his language,
Which I didn't understand.
He made his words a symbol
As he gestured with his hands.

His style was stern but gentle,
And he taught me as a child.
I came to love this human,
Who was ever strong, but mild.

I learned to watch and listen;
Each command I came to know.
My progress came quite quickly.
My training began to show.

Soon I learned to sit and fetch,
And heel at my master's feet.
I made my master happy
But my task was not complete.

Whistles were my next command,
Along with voice inflection.
This taught me to read his mind;
To move at his direction.

Learning as the weeks went by
I began to feel quite grand!
Working was a partnership,
Dog and cowboy; paw and hand!

I've since passed all my training,
And I work hard every day.
Trying to please my master
As I strive to earn my pay.

So now if it's a gesture,
Or a whistle shrill and loud,
I know what he wants of me
And I try to make him proud.

See, I'm a Border Collie,
Working stock is what I do.
Learnin' how to help my man
Is what I'm s'posed to do.

We've worked so much together,
Now I catch him by surprise.
His thoughts are 'bout plain as day,
I can see them in his eyes.

He enters in th' tack room
And I catch him with my stare.
With one quick look I ask him ....
"Should I go and get the mare?"

MARE AND COLT

SECOND CHANCE

Written By

Sam DeLeeuw

Oh, what a life to be the wife
Of a rancher raisin' horses.
On fertile land we run a band,
With the best of all resources.

Sweet Lucerne hay in breezes sway
A full three crops we cut and bail.
Clear sparklin' streams with sunlight beams
Roll through our pastures filled with quail.

There was a time in this sublime
When my ranch life was not serene.
When sickness reigned and nine months drained
All skin color, exceptin' green.

New life ordains strong labor pains,
It was my time to deliver!
Can't find the Doc! Then comes a knock!
It's our vet from up the river.

"Invite him in!" said with a grin,
"Mark it as a broodmare preg-check!
Oh, bless my soul, I'm gonna foal!"
That's when my husband hit the deck!

When he came to, the birth was through.
Chance was cradled in my embrace.
Thanks to our vet you sure could bet
We'd remember this time and place!

As was our rule he'd go to school,
Obtain a medical degree.
And all the while we would just smile,
"We'll get our doctorin' fer free!"

Well, late one night, by lantern light
When checkin' Queen, our fav'rite mare,
We heard the moans and throaty groans.
A breach birth was happening there.

"On the double, Queen's in trouble!
Call Chance and get him on the phone!"
When mares are due, the vets are few.
You're foalin' mares out on your own.

Chance soon arrives our foal survives
And he's a good one we can see
Marks like his paw, head like his maw,
Future champ is the guarantee!

A breach is grim, if not for him
We would have lost both foal and mare.
But there he stood and all was good
For Queen and baby sucklin' there.

Strange to say one other day
Chance was delivered by a vet.
For what it's worth, suppose this birth
Could be the payment for that debt!

To pick a name, a good one came
With no more than a sidelong glance
It's plain to see the name must be…
What else? Queen's Little Second Chance.

ANDALUSIAN

RETIRED

Written By
Skylar Harwood

You say that I'm retired
but I'm still in my prime
The day may come to call me old
but it's not yet that time

I'm agile as a yearling
I slide stop, run and turn
That buckle you wear on your belt
is one I helped you earn

Now I'm locked up in this barn
well groomed with proper care
But to end my days of being rode
is not the least bit fair

That young horse that your riding
has a real good pedigree
But if your wanting to win big
You oughtta saddle me

I spin just like a dradle
with a cue from just your feet
No need to move the reins on me
Just leave em hanging neat

I know your gonna miss me
if you don't already now
Whether when your out there reining
or ya wanna cut a cow

You no doubt like my genetics
cause you know their fit to win
which brings up this complaint I have
and the fix you've left me in

You had me bred by my competitor
Who I more times have beat
In hopes my foal's a champion
who's strong and fast and neat

You're probably right on that account
This colt will sure be fine
But don't ya think a baby
is a choice that should be mine

This is gonna be a lot of work
more so than rodeoing
I never would have guessed
that this is where my life was going

I should be turned out to pasture
free to run just being fed
You tell me I'm retired
So why the Hell'd you get me bred

HAPPY TRAILS AND PONY TAILS

REST STOP

Written By
Phil Ellsworth

We left that morning before the sun,
For one of the tougher circles on our range.
It was a long ride from headquarters,
But the weather was nice for a change.

By noon we'd bunched our gather,
In a swale about halfway home.
It seemed a good time for a break,
And give the horses a chance to rest some.

Once in a while your mind takes pictures,
Of scenes you'll always remember.
That's the way it was for me that day,
I think it was late September.

Four tired horses standing together,
Cropping grass on a little strip of green,
While we riders go hunt some shade.
And rustle our lunch bags and canteens.

We took our rest and the horses took theirs,
And it made for a better trip home,
Tho' it was after dark when we got there,
The lights from the ranch cheered us some.

I guess the picture stays with me,
Tho' it was a long time ago.
Because we four friends and those four horses,
Never rode together again.

BLUE SHAWL

WRAPPED IN LOVE

Written By
Gary Penney

I came across a picture
Taken forty years ago.
The picture was my mother.
You could see her youthful glow.

She wore a skirt of turquoise
And a blouse of snowy white;
A blue shawl draped around her
And her hair was combed just right.

The shawl had been a present
Given on her wedding day.
She'd shared it with her children
In a very special way.

I gazed upon this picture
And my eyes filled up with tears.
I thought of all the good times
That we'd had throughout the years.

A hardy Western woman
With a dedicated life.
She'd been the perfect mother
And a most deserving wife.

She'd raised six lovely daughters
And a lone endearing son.
Her work seemed never ending
Yet, she could never be outdone.

She was our daddy's helpmate
Workin' cows and breakin' sod.
Time was made for each of us
But her Sundays went to God.

She read her Holy Bible
The way that we all ought.
Her life would be a lesson
Of how we should all be taught.

We were raised on hope and faith
With our God's love from above.
It bound us all together
As a family filled with love.

She'd call us kids together
And take that old blue shawl,
Wrap us in her loving arms
And make each of us feel small.

Even when we left her home
And took jobs earning wages,
We were still her babies
Regardless of our ages.

We'd all come back to visit
Though with time it got real sad.
Her mind had started failing
And her health was turning bad.

Father Time had come a callin'
As he's always apt to do.
He'd tapped her on the shoulder,
Said, "This time I've come for you."

The last time that I saw her
She was peaceful in her bed.
She looked directly at me
And this is what she said;

"You know that I've been ready
And I've heard God softly call...,"
"Come to me my loving child.
Let Me wrap you in My shawl."

LOOKING BACK

REFLECTIONS

Written By
Gary Penney

I've finished riding fences
And the cattle are all fine.
No troubles found for the day
So the evening is all mine.

I rest atop my pony
And reflect upon the day.
Then I ponder to myself,
Who else might have passed this way?

I gaze towards the mountains
Through this prairie thick with grass.
I think about the buffalo
And a time that's long since passed.

Mustangs from Conquistadors
Ran wild throughout those canyons.
The Red Man caught and trained them
To be their true companions.

I can almost see the teepees
Where the weeping willows grow.
Beside the flowing waters
Lived the Cheyenne, Sioux, and Crow.

Then I see a wagon train
With settl'rs brave and bold.

They seek fortunes in the West
With great hopes of finding gold.

I hear the hooves of Longhorns
From a ghostly cattle drive.
Charlie Goodnight passed this way
To bring cattle where they thrive.

I can't forget young cowboys
Who got tough along the way.
I owe my job to their grit
And I'm thankful every day.

Do I hear a distant hammer
Pounding posts out on the range?
'Tis the stringing of the wire
That will bring about a change.

Buffalo have disappeared
And the Red Men all have moved.
Charlie Goodnight's long since gone,
But he would have disapproved.

Old trails are paved with concrete.
The wagons now are rotten.
Open range is all fenced in;
True pioneers forgotten.

I guess I'm just a dreamer
As I see things from the past.
I think back to olden days
And of things that did not last.

I'm so thankful to the folks
Who blazed the trail for me.
They make my life seem easy
Raisin' cows and livin' free.

Now the sun is settin' low
And the skies are changing hue.
Heaven's turning red and orange.
It's come time to bid adieu.

I thank you Lord for this time
With reflections that will last.
You've brightened up my future
By my looking to the past.

FULL OF BULL

PRODDY MAMMA

Written By

Sam DeLeeuw

The cutest is black face babies
Come calvin' time in early spring.
But some of them proddy mamas
Would fit in a bull fightin' ring

Nothin' more protective, raunchy,
Than a black hearted Angus cow,
When you're tryin' to tag her calf
While staying uninjured somehow.

Do not think of bringin' a dog,
It only makes these matters worse.
She'll take him on, he'll skedaddle,
Only to yelp and then reverse.

For safety he now runs to you,
Drops and cowers behind your heels.
Head down, Old Mama takes dead aim!
Through red eyes her hate she reveals.

The dog takes off! You're left to fend!
End up astride her thick black neck!
Ear tags and needles go flyin',
Thus beginin' a mad cow wreck!

One hoof splatters the iodine,
Another, the combiotic,
Taggin' gun soars right, bottles left,
As Mama becomes psychotic!

Your legs are wrapped around her eyes
She flings you up and then around.
You snatch her tail as you fly by
As you are slammed into the ground.

She scoops you up across her nose!
At once, propels you one more time
About ten feet into the air,
Then grinds your body in the slime.

At least you are back on the ground
Until that dog begins to bark.
He heads that cow right back to you!
As you glance up, the world goes dark!

Comin' to, you see Old Mama
Cuddlin' up her black bull calf.
A sidelong stare you can't describe.
Through cracked ribs you begin to laugh.

How she feels about your presence,
This Witch has made extremely clear.
She isn't afraid to take you on
And again slam you on your rear!

Tomorrow, you'll bring the squeeze chute,
Couple of horses and more men.
Tie up the dog, corner the calf,
Rope and drag Mama to the pen.

There really are easier ways
To accomplish this task each spring.
Sheesh! Just do it right the first time,
Thus, avoiding that body sling!

WILD AND FREE

CHALLENGING THE WIND

Written By
Ol' Jim Cathey

Crisp air at early mornin' light, a band of mustangs in full flight,
cascade down the steep mountain trail.
Smoothly flow thru rock an' tree, racin' down so gracefully,
yet ever cautious as they sail.

Collage of colors flashin' by, playful yearlings cavort an' fly,
an' squeal with pretended wrath.
While matriarchs nip their flanks, to calm their youthful, snortin' pranks,
an' keep 'em headed on their path.

The ponies, shinin' in the sun, swept down the valley at a run,
headin' fer the sweet mesa grass.
Their hoof beats clattered on the rock, these ponies from good mustang stock,
visions of beauty as they pass.

The leaders set a torrid pace; stragglers try to stay the race,
runnin' as if they had been spurred.
The thunderin' hooves pound the earth, as dust clouds experience birth,
to then hang behind the herd.

They move as one thru rocks an' draws, a fluid beast that will not pause,
until they reach their final goal.
Beauty of speed an' flowin' manes, poundin' hooves leave loud refrains,
a deep melodious drum roll.

At meadows edge, there lies a pool, with waters clear an' mountain cool,
invitin' them to quench their thirst.
They slow an' spread along the marge, to drink their fill an' thus recharge,
most with muzzels now immersed.

One by one they break away, for meadow graze an' maybe play,
a ritual for one to see.
Ponies spread out far an' wide, watchful patriarch on the side,
alert for danger constantly.

Evenin' shadows start to grow, ponies bunch as if they know,
darkness develops its own plight.
The stallion's signal rings out shrill; he'll safely push them up the hill,
an' then to guard them thru the night.

He will circle, nippin' at flanks, so they tighten up the ranks,
he knows he can protect them then.
As mornin' sun will heat the day, afternoon slowly fades away,
an' darkness settles on the glen.

An' they know that they are free!

A TAIL OF PROTECTION

IT SEEMS LIKE ONLY YESTERDAY

Written By

Daniel Dobson

It seems like only yesterday.

I remember when you were born
I could've asked for nothing more
A healthy happy baby boy
that needed only me.

And then when you began to walk
I was so proud, and then you talked.
At first no one could understand you.
No one except for me.

It seems like only yesterday.

I recall just how fast you grew
You were one, then you were too.
But still you needed comforting
A job for only me.

And when you began to jump and play
Watch me mom! Is what you'd say.
No one else you seem to notice
no one except for me.

It seems like only yesterday.

I remember that shy colt I knew
Hiding behind me a time or two.
In need of my protecting
A treasure for only me.

And you made friends at every turn
I was surprised at how much you learned.
And you were great at everything
a joy shared by me.

It seems like only yesterday.

I recall meeting your loving mate.
You knew that she was your true fate.
It's what I always hoped for you
A prayer answered for me.

Now I pray she always treats you good
And put you first just like I would
And know the world begins and ends with you
For a mother just like me.

But it still seems like only yesterday.

THE FIDDLER

BEER STAINS IN THE WOOD

Written By
Gary Penney

This happened at a shindig
On a Friday night in May.
We'd gone there for the music
And to dance the night away.

They had a little string band
And a cowboy that could sing.
Their music filled the rafters
With old tunes and Western Swing.

I loved their cowboy fiddler.
(You could tell he'd been around.)
He could saw those fiddle strings
To enhance that Western sound.

But then I got all puzzled
By a question in my head.
I sauntered up beside him
And this is what I said;

"I guess I've always wondered,
So help me solve this riddle.
What seems to be th' difference
'Tween a violin and fiddle?"

I thought that I had stumped him
'Til he calmly lit a smoke.
He shared his cowboy wisdom.
So, I listened as he spoke.

"While a violin is pretty
With it's varnish and its shine
A fiddle just makes music
To keep beat in cowboy time.

Violins will do the same
And might sometimes sound as good.
But, here's th' diff'rence 'tween th' two……
It's called beer stains in th' wood.

Cowboys love their honky tonks
Where the beer just seems to flow.
That's where you'll find a fiddler
Playing Western songs you know.

But sometimes there are problems
When the beer has flowed too long.
Seems those cowboys want to fight
And stop listenin' to your song.

Say adieu to "Faded Love";
Goodbye to "Cotton Eyed Joe".
Beer comes sailing by your ear
And you know it's time to go.

You rush to pack your fiddle
While retrieving tips and cash.
Time has come to hit the road.
Then it hits you…….. with a SPLASH!

Luke warm beer runs down your hat
While you sigh a sad refrain.
You know that poor ol' fiddle
Just acquired another stain.

Now, here's my little secret
That shows I've been around.
There's somethin' 'bout a beer stain
That adds richness to the sound.

Violins can play the music
And might sometimes sound as good.
But Western Swing sounds better
When there's beer stains in the wood."

NO FRILLS

SASS-Y SHOOTER

Written By
Sam DeLeeuw

Today's Single Action Shooting,
A Society in the West.
They gather to test marksmanship.
By *Trails End*, they're at their best!

They vie all year, 'cross the Nation
Endin' up at this final shoot.
'Longside others, they'll pit their skills
For the title that's in dispute.

This SASS-y Shooter does not take
A second stance to any man.
Standing calm, she will draw then shoot.
Her rapid shots she'll deftly fan.

These contests don't intimidate.
"COWGIRL UP!" is her driving creed.
She steps to the line, sets her jaw,
Poised to react with viper speed.

During one shoot or another,
She has been challenged by the best.
She stands her ground, she holds her own,
To be a "Woman of the West."

It's not ego behind her smile,
Just raw self-confidence and pride.
Not only can she draw and shoot,
But she can swing aboard and ride.

In shooting from a running horse,
She's just as "dead on" in her aim
As with her holstered forty-five.
Rifle… pistol… it's all the same.

She shoots with either right or left,
Brandishing her balanced spinners.
She'll show her style, her top notch skill,
As she stands among the winners.

The boys would like to win her heart,
Win her hand, if she would let them.
But they won't even win this shoot.
That's their first and foremost problem!

Oh someday, maybe, she'll relent,
Put down her rifle and her gun.
But not today! It's *Trails End*!
This is it and it's all or none!

She tells the boys to "bring it on!"
Sends a challenge to all shooters.
They can be her partners today,
But in no way be her suitors!

She nods to all, then draws and shoots!
She makes her point in cowgirl style.
This SASS-y Shooter gives the boys
…A wink and understated smile.

BEAUTY AND GRACE

BEAUTY OF THE SOUL

Written By
Gary Penney

I'm just a workin' cowboy,
Or at least I used to be.
Living on the open range
Was the kind of life for me.

But....., God reached out and touched me.
He said, *"This is not for you.*
You're gonna be My artist
And it's what you're meant to do.

I'll fill your hand with talent
Sharing beauty that you see.
You'll put it all on canvas
And be painting just for Me.

I want to see some horses
With perhaps some elk or deer.
Paint some cowboys by a fire
Singing melodies of cheer.

I love silhouettes of cacti
In the sunset as it wains.
Paint insects in their flowers
After soothing springtime rains.

My snow-capped peaks are awesome
With their clouds of puffy white.
Add in some streaks of sunshine
To reveal My wondrous might.

And don't forget My people
With expressions on each face.
I'll help you with the details
To exude My love and grace."

So....., God blessed me with this talent
That I'll never understand.
My eyes can see an image
And transfer it to my hand.

But now I faced a challenge
That I'd never faced before.
I set out to paint the face
Of my wife, whom I adore.

I spread the paint on canvas
Mixing colors of each hue.
I felt His Holy presence
As we saw this project through.

I can't paint unselfishness
Or the kindness of a heart.
She gives so much to others
That she sets herself apart.

Her soul is filled with sunshine
With His grace from up above.
Her kindness, love and mercy
Truly fill my home with love.

I painted in some softness
With her hair of shining gold.
I drew in a cowboy hat
Just to add a touch of bold.

God worked on eyes and sparkle
And the glory in her face.
His touch enhanced her beauty
Mixing elegance with grace.

So now my portrait's finished
And I think I've met my goal.
I've shown her earthly features
While God's magnified her soul.

CORRAL CUTIES

SISTERS

Written By

Sam DeLeeuw

Jamie, brown eyes and auburn hair.
Geri, blonde, eyes of blazing blue.
Sisters, the same but different.
One lady, one more buckaroo.

The lady clad in boots and dress,
Was still a cowgirl just the same.
She tied goats, roped and ran barrels.
Felt when a horse was goin' lame.

Now a veterinarian,
Years while tending horses, she learned.
Experience was her teacher.
Her reputation has been earned.

The little blue-eyed buckaroo
Grew with the horses just as well.
She was aggressive when she rode.
She"d whip-n-spur and rode pell-mell!

Obtained a degree in nursing,
Cares for the two legged critter.
Bringing human babies to earth,
Evermore, a baby-sitter.

Both rodeo queens, many times.
Rode young horses with gentle hands.
Learned what effort at school would bring
And what success in life demands.

They didn't always get along.
Now and then, they quarreled and fought.
From this was learned understanding,
And patience was usually taught.

Sisters, the same but so diff'rent.
Unlike in hues of eyes and hair.
The same in beliefs and in creeds,
All God's creations need their care.

Jamie, brown eyes and auburn hair.
Geri, blonde, eyes of blazing blue.
Sisters, the same but different.
One lady, one more buckaroo.

DESERT ROUNDUP

DESERT YEARLIN'S

Written By
Sam DeLeeuw

Sorrels, grays, dapples, bays
Came crashing through the brush,
Raising clouds, dusty shrouds
With skies in crimson blush.

Ropes aloft, voices soft,
Vaqueros run the herd.
Morning air coats the hair,
Their racing legs are blurred.

With each spring, Vaqueros bring
The yearlin's to be sold.
Desert bred, fully shed,
Their values met in gold.

Riders know, there's no whoa
Each day they're workin' stock.
Inborn sense, their best defense,
Sidesteppin' lichened rock.

Fleet of hoof, certain proof
The best is desert bred.
Each careens through ravines
Chasin' cows that's desert fed.

At wild pace, yearlin's race
Until they reach the pens.
Picks are made, money laid
In hundreds, fives and tens.

Sorrels, grays, dapples, bays
Broken by vaqueros.
Desert born, no brands worn,
Purchased with deneros.

Papers signed, colts consigned.
Vaqueros start for home.
This year's foals meet their goals,
On desert plains they roam.

Yearlin's sold, coyotes scold,
Skies turn to crimson blush.
Sorrels, grays, dapples, bays
Trail homeward through the brush.

PICK ME PICK ME

ROSE AND DOLLY

Written By
Gary Penney

As I recall my childhood
And my time on Granddad's farm
I can't forget two donkeys
With great character and charm.

He'd bought 'em for the grandkids,
For our pleasure and our play.
They gave us all sweet mem'ries
We recall until this day.

Their names were Rose and Dolly.
They were really quite a pair.
You could tell they loved us kids
And were glad when we were there.

When we'd go out to visit
They'd come greet us at the gate.
They'd bray, snort and paw the dirt.
You could tell they couldn't wait.

These two were, oh, so gentle
That they never brought us harm.
It made our days seem special
With our playtimes on the farm.

Dolly liked to pull our cart
That was made by Granddad's hands.
He'd made it from scrap lumber
Without ever using plans.

The boys would go out riding
Playing cowboys all the way.
We'd fight off all attackers
And be heroes for the day.

The girls played near the shade tree
As they spent their days with Rose.
They'd dress her with a bed sheet
And put lipstick on her nose.

She'd sometimes wear a bonnet,
If the girls could all agree.
You should have heard the giggles
Come from underneath that tree.

These donkeys were our playmates
Dressing up or pulling carts.
We cherished their sweet friendship
As they stole away our hearts.

We wiled away the hours
In our imaginations.
These donkeys were so patient
They needed commendations.

They always got rewarded
With a rubdown and a snack.
Their favorites were the carrots
And cubed sugar from a sack.

Looking back upon our time
With these friends from long ago
I remember sweet goodbyes
Just before we had to go.

When we loaded up the car
And prepared to drive away,
Rose and Dolly both cut up
And would loudly stomp and bray.

They said in donkey language,
"We enjoyed our afternoon.
We can't wait to play again
And we hope to see you soon!!!"

ED

THE MASTER'S HAND

Written By
Richard Wright

With gentle touch the calm returns,
She seems to understand;
The horse can sense there's love within
The master's gentle hand.

In younger years he rode the range,
An outfit in Cheyenne;
He found a gift for horsemanship,
A calling soon began.

He wasn't much for bustin' broncs,
He tried a gentler tack;
A talk, a walk, a saddle eased,
He gave the reins some slack.

He grew to know their temperament,
The way a horse will tell
If happy, angry, lonesome, bored,
Or just not feeling well.

Once he drove a herd up north
To Bozeman in the fall;
Got caught up in an early snow,
But still delivered all.

And once while east of Omaha
While caught out in the rain,
He delivered a newborn foal,
And eased her momma's pain.

So many years in the saddle,
Some good ones and some bad;
They'll always be a part of him,
Both happy times and sad.

His skin is more like leather now,
His brow is lined with age;
He feels the days are growing short,
But knows he's earned his wage.

And even now in sunset years
It seems a small demand,
Allowing equine friends to feel
The master's gentle hand.

FISHING WITH GRANDPA

HOOKED

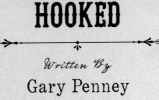

Written By
Gary Penney

Today my Princess visits,
And I'll treat her like a Queen.
She'll get a royal treatment
Unlike one she's ever seen.

The last time that I saw her
She expressed a special wish.
"Next time I come to visit.....
Can you take me out to fish?"

My heart almost exploded
As my chest swelled up with pride.
"Of course I'll take you, Sweetie!"
Then I almost up and cried.

Though she's only six years old
She can put you right at ease.
She's got a sense of humor
That can bring you to your knees.

I don't think she's held a worm.
She's not handled reel or pole.
The fish don't need to know that
When we hit my fav'rite hole.

We boated to some willows
Where we pulled up in the shade.
I think we'd found some water
Where a "big one" may have strayed.

I opened up a carton
Of night crawlers in some peat.
When it comes to catching perch
This ol' fav'rite's hard to beat.

Princess starts to make a face
When I string one on the hook.
I said, "That's the way to do it."
Then she flashed her "funky" look.

I tossed him in the water
And in no more than a flash
She had hooked a big ol' perch
That began to fight and thrash.

The battle soon was over
As she claimed the victory.
I snapped her cheesy picture;
Not for her.... but more for ME!

This scene was oft' repeated
As she tallied up her score.
I'd bet in one full hour
She caught twenty-five, or more!

By now our day was over
And I hadn't caught a one.
I'd been busy helping her......,
Catching fish and having fun!

This didn't go unnoticed,
So my Princess made a joke.
She spun her sense of humor
With child's laughter as she spoke.

"Next time I come to see you
Will you grant another wish?
Show me how to ride a horse......;
And I'll teach *you* how to fish!"

DESERT DELIVERY

A WESTERN ICON

Written By
Ol' Jim Cathey

It came to life in eighteen sixty,
this plan to deliver the mail.
Good horses and young tough riders
would go skitterin' acrost that trail.

Now, to fetch mail from Saint Joe
to that gold country way out there,
shore 'nuff took a spell by stagecoach.
Quicker than a month was mighty rare!

So these fellers got the idea
to deliver it by horseback,
runnin' hard for about ten mile,
then put a fresh horse on the track.

They'd need several stations,
an' a staff of mighty tough men,
just to ride those wiry mounts
held ready, there in that pen.

The miles they'd need to cover,
gave many a danger an' snare.
'Cuz often, wild savage would lurk,
an' the weather was bad out there.

Always ridin' at breakneck speed,
acrost perilous, unmarked trails,
proved tough on both rider an' mount,
givin' birth to heroic tales.

Tales that would live thru spoken word,
with many a campfire narration.
Told, tho memory often blurred,
as new tales found their creation.

'Course, good ideas sometime fall apart
when you deal with other's desires.
Here comes progress in eighteen months,
in the form of telegraph wires!

So, the Pony Express was short lived,
but it made its mark on this land.
An' became an icon of the West,
to stay around for a spell as a brand.

Wal, this made such an impression,
as pilgrims crossed the western states,
that most of the major stations
were re-enactment advocates.

Thus, pageants an' shows would get a start,
as the glory of this dangerous quest
would show valor, heart, an' courage,
of men an' horses of the West.

An' its memory is often kept alive,
thru romanticism an' mystery.
These dashing young riders portray,
moments relived in western history.

With all the flair they could contrive,
thru gallant horses an' brave men,
They kept this memory alive.
Pony Express would ride again!

SUNLIT COWBOY

COWBOY POETS

Written by Leslie V. Bay

From sun up to sun down, day in and day out, the cowboy hears stories whispering all around them. Whispers that may be a family member telling them stories of their lives on the great open range. Stories come through many paths, like the voices that may be faintly heard as the wind swirls around, howling out history during a cattle drive. Those voices may be real or they may be the echoes of long ago.

Voices and real life experiences are what give us, the reader, a glimpse into one of the most cherished traditions to ever pass this great land, that of the Cowboy Poets, hurling the familiar lasso. The Lasso that Captures The West in Art.

Sit back in your saddle and get ready for one of the most memorable rides of your life, as you read about the great Cowboy Poets of the West inspired by the Art of Marless Fellows.

⟡ ★ ⟡

Ol' Jim Cathey

About Ol' Jim Cathey

From the Heart of Texas, and he prefers to be called Ol' Jim. Growing up on a ranch in Erath County, Ol' Jim found his love for the land, horses, cattle, and naturally...the cowboy way of life. According to Ol' Jim, "I've been married for 50 years...to the same woman, my young bride Stella! We both have degrees from Texas A&M University, have two children and a passel of grandkids."

Becoming A Cowboy Poet

"I always loved cowboy stories and western lore as told by my Granddad, Papa Hop. Papa Hop spent a lot of time telling stories of his life on the Panhandle Plains of Texas. When I retired I began writing," says Ol' Jim.

"I began to write my own original poetry and currently have written 122 poems. In 2009 and 2010, I entered the National Cowboy Poetry Rodeo in Montrose, CO. There I competed with other cowboy poets. I was encouraged as I placed third and fourth in the four events both years. The NCPR moved to Kanab, Utah for 2011 and 2012. I had three first place finishes in 2012 and won the Silver Buckle and the All-Around Champion Award. I have 12 poems published on cowboypoetry.com and write a newspaper column called 'On The Back Porch' where I discuss our Western Heritage and include one of my original poems," Ol' Jim continues.

What makes being a cowboy so ingrained in your life that it leads you to poetry?

Ol' Jim says, "Growing up in rural Texas and living the western cowboy and ranching life, I experienced the good times, as well as the hard times. This taught me an appreciation for how nature and the land affect people and animals. Being surrounded by God's beauty and His bounty helped me develop an inner sense that helped me understand about life and God's plan for me."

Who is your favorite cowboy poet?

"I have made so many friends since 2007. Many are very good at cowboy poetry. But, it's hard to top the old classic cowboy poetry. I really like the works of S. Omar Barker. I have committed several of his poems to memory and have received permission from his foundation to use his poems," Ol' Jim remembers.

What inspires you about Marless' artwork?

Ol' Jim remarks, "Marless has captured the essence of the western way of life, with many of her works portraying hidden aspects and behind the scenes images that are the meat of our western heritage. She exhibits a feeling for the way it is, instead of a glamorized West."

What is the one thing you want to share with people in your poetry?

"Basically the same thing Marless does with her art. I want people to get a feel for the real western way of life, the same thing people experienced growing up, surviving, and understanding what life is really about. At the same time, I want to help people see the humorous side of life, although much of my work tends to be on the serious side. I want people to have a feel for how God, in all His infinite wisdom was able to provide a balance and a harmony for life as it is meant to be experienced," Ol' Jim imparts.

One Great Ride and with Whom?

"Now this one is easy, it would be Charlie Goodnight on a cattle drive up the Chisholm Trail!"

Keep Yer Powder Dry!! Ol' Jim

Jim Cathey ★ onejcat@sbcglobal.net ★ www.bootsnrhymes.com

SAM DeLeeuw

About Sam DeLeeuw

Born in Blackfoot, Idaho, Sam rode the Ft. Hall Reservation with her dad. According to Sam, "He gave me my first horse, Stormy, a quarter horse mare, when I was four. Before then I rode double with my dad on his big horse, Red, hanging on to his belt loops."

Sam remembers, "Dad said he was the only father in town that sent a daughter, two horses and a dog to college. I attended Snow College in Ephraim, Utah, and was one of two girls in Feeds and Feeding and Livestock Selection. I graduated from Utah State University with a secondary degree in Physical Education."

"I taught school, then went on to be a juvenile probation officer in Manti, Utah. After 30 plus years I retired and moved to Roy, Utah, where I currently reside. During that time I have been on the Sanpete County Fair Board for over 30 years, chaired the Rodeo Queens, taught horse 4-H for over 25 years and was the President of the Utah State Fairs and Events Association," says Sam.

Sam has two daughters and eight grandchildren.

Becoming A Cowboy Poet

According to Sam, "I have written prose all my life, but started writing poetry later. My daughters were rodeo queens, several times over and it was easier to remember their speeches if they rhymed. I then created HILDA THE TRAIL DRIVE CAMP COOK and from there, it is history. Hilda has taken me many places and allowed me a myriad of experiences."

What makes being a cowboy so ingrained in your life that it leads you to poetry?

Sam insists, "I am not a cowboy, but this cowGIRL has branded, castrated, trailed cows and enjoyed every minute of it.

I was a popular 'date' at college at branding time, you see. I can brand, inoculate, dehorn or whatever else is needed. And I love Rocky Mtn. Oysters!!!!! I was married for 20 years to a man who had cows and sheep and from that came many 'escapades' that turned into stories! I write about what I see, what I feel, what I have experienced. Working the land and working stock is a good way to live."

Who is my favorite cowboy poet?

"Don Kennington, Utah cowboy poet, now retired. I listened to his words and I watched how he presented his material. He could have you rolling in the aisles with laughter and in the next story wiping tears of emotion. What a great teacher and a wonderful man," relates Sam.

What inspires you about Marless' artwork?

"It is real! Each new picture brings back memories in my life. Most of the pictures, I can say 'I'VE BEEN THERE, DONE THAT!' Cows, horses, sheep, old cowboys, great cowgirls, friends, neighbors and rides are all represented in her artwork," says Sam.

One thing I want to share in my poetry?

Sam expresses, "I would really like to tap some of their memories (or imaginations) and bring them to life. I want to touch their funny bones or their hearts."

One Great Ride and with Whom?

Sam recalls, "One of these days, Bill and I will return to the Wind River area in Wyoming. We both have been there, but not together. It's one of my favorite places to ride and camp. It would be my dream to share it with the one I love so much! Working the land and working stock is a good way to live."

Sam DeLeeuw ★ samcowgalpoet@aol.com ★ www.cowgalpoet.com

DANIEL DOBSON

About Daniel Dobson
This is one man who was "lasso'd" by Marless Fellows you see, Dan Dobson is her son and it's a family tradition. That family history for the love of the Wild West was sent down the family chain and captured Dan, just like it captured Marless Fellows. Dan is a 32 year-old farmer out of Gilbert, Arizona, following in his father's footsteps. Although farming is his profession, Dan also is a singer-songwriter and enjoys reading and writing poetry.

Becoming A Cowboy Poet
According to Dan, "My main influences are Shakespeare and Edgar Allen Poe. I feel my poetry is a success when the reader gets some emotion from reading the poetry. My dad is also a poet and that was a great influence as well."

Growing up in the same cowboy way that Fellows did, has also influenced this young farmer to carry on the family traditions and bare his soul in his writing.

What makes being a cowboy so ingrained in your life that it leads you to poetry?
Dan says, "As I like to say I am really a farmer with spurs on! Actually growing up in Arizona and coming from a family well-known for being cowboys and farmers, it was hard not to write your feelings. Of course, my mom's father and grandfather gave me the best of both worlds."

You can't help but pick all that up and start to write down your feelings from the ground up, starts in your feet and goes right to your head!

Who is my favorite cowboy poet?
"I really don't have just one favorite poet as I am inspired daily by authors of long ago as well as today. Just looking around at the vast land that surrounds me is inspiration and then I pick up a pen," says Dan.

What inspires you about Marless' artwork?
Dan relates, "Mom has an eye for creating the slow paced country life in her art. I also love how in most of her pieces you can find people enjoying simple pleasures such as the company of others or the companionship of a simple horse or dog."

One thing I want to share in my poetry?
"Just as my mom has done in this book I want to share what the Cowboy Way has meant to my whole family over the generations, I do that in my song and my verse," says Dan Dobson.

One Great Ride and with Whom?
Dan's memories of his grandfathers are as strong as his mom's. In Dan's words, "If I could go on a trail ride with any two people I would go with both my grandfathers. I would talk to my grandfather Earl Dobson about his life in farming when he was young, and then I would take a quick detour with my grandfather John Buchanan down by Roosevelt Lake, grab a fishing pole and spend the afternoon reliving some of my fondest memories."

PHIL ELLSWORTH

About Phil Ellsworth
Dr. Phil Ellsworth said he had been a horse lover all of his life. He got his first horse at the age of 13 when his family purchased a few acres on a ranch in Middle Park, Colorado. It took three summers to build the log cabin and he and his brother began irrigating for local ranches and taking guests on trail rides. A few years later he was starting colts and doing some of the shoeing.

Before graduating from vet school, he worked at a feedlot in Greeley, CO that fed about 40,000 head. Phil practiced in Safford for three and a half years after a couple of years in the Army. It was mostly cattle and horse practice. After that, he purchased a practice in Prescott, AZ and continued in horse and cattle work as well as small animals.

Becoming a Cowboy Poet
He says, his mother had a gift for rhyming and he may have picked up some of that. After selling his practice, he began writing about some of the adventures of veterinary work and was involved in some of the early work of putting a Poet Gathering together in Prescott. There he met the Abbotts and later purchased a horse from them and was invited to work some of their round-ups. He liked nothing better than hunting cows in rough country. Since he was small he liked it when his Father recited the "Cremation of Sam McGee," by Robert W. Service.

Who is your favorite poet?
"I really admire Rolf Flake, and my favorite poem is one by Sunny Hancock called 'The Horse Trade' that Rolf recites to a T."

What inspires you about Marless' artwork?
"Marless has a real talent and her art shows the modern west. When I see some of the pictures, a story comes to mind and I use it as a foundation for the poem," says Phil.

What is the one thing you want to share in your poetry?
"Showing the 'glamour' of veterinary practice and a little about Prescott's history," relays Phil.

One Great Ride and with Whom?
"The ride I remember the most was a round-up with Abbots on the P Bar at Parks. Mary and I ended up on drag and had stopped at the top of a swale with 400 some black cows moving down the swale and up the other side. They were three or four abreast and stretched out close to half a mile with the San Francisco Peaks in the background. It reminded me of a smaller version of the old cattle drives. You guessed it. No camera," remembers Phil.

Phil Ellsworth ★ jpedvm@aol.com

105

GREG HARWOOD

About Greg Harwood

As Greg likes to say, he started "cowboying" at the age of 16 where he worked for a feedlot during the winter and lived on the mountain with the cow herd during the summer. By age 21, Greg married and recently celebrated their 32nd anniversary. Greg and his wife have four children and four grandchildren.

According to Greg, "I cowboyed for several years after we married, I also learned how to auctioneer and have been selling cattle every Tuesday at our local auction barn for the last 30 years."

Greg has had a long career as a law enforcement officer in Utah, where he has lived and worked for the last 24 years. The last 11 years of his tenure were spent as the police chief in Salina, UT. Greg recently retired but not for long as he was re-hired as our local school resource officer.

How did you become a Cowboy Poet?

According to Greg, "I began by helping my children with English assignments at school, I also wrote poems about my grandparents which I read at their funerals. My son Skylar started writing poetry in middle school and won a contest which allowed him the opportunity to entertain during a Baxter Black concert. Since then he has been asked to entertain at several cowboy gatherings including Durango, CO and Heber City, UT. Once Skylar got busy with his poetry he encouraged me to continue to write."

So I guess you can say this one a little differently, "Like son, like father" for Skylar and Greg!

What makes being a cowboy so ingrained in your life that it leads you to poetry?

Greg believes, "Being a cowboy is an occupation as well as a lifestyle. In today's world, opportunities to make your living as a cowboy are quite limited and becoming even more scarce. I hate to think of a world without cowboys. Cowboy poetry is my small contribution to keeping the cowboy way of life alive."

Who is my favorite cowboy poet?

"I have two favorite poets; my son Skylar is my favorite poet as I always enjoy his poetry and his unique way of delivering a poem. An old timer from Northern Utah named Don Kennington is another of my favorites, especially his poem *Shoein' Old Rivet*," recalls Greg.

What inspires you about Marless' artwork?

"Marless is certainly a talented artist. With each painting I can think of someone I know who the painting reminds me of, or, of a time in my past of a specific place or event that happened in my life," says Greg.

What's the one thing you want to share with people in your poetry?

Greg relates, "It's fun to be able to paint a picture with words and help the listener put himself in the story where they can see and feel what I am seeing and feeling. It's a bonus when the story is comical or can make the listener feel good."

If you could take one great ride, who would it be with and where would you go?

Says Greg, "I have a busy schedule so a great ride for me is any time I get the chance to help our local ranchers gather cattle from the mountain late in the fall around late October or early November. Gathering cattle in the Seven-Mile/Boobe Hole country or under the White Mountain up Salina Creek is a great ride, especially when I get to ride with my family or friends."

Greg Harwood ★ g.harwood@hotmail.com

SKYLAR HARWOOD

About Skylar Harwood

Skylar Harwood was born and raised in central Utah. Skylar still lives in central Utah with his wife Brandi and their two sons, KC Cinch and Riggin Cole. Skylar likes to ride horses, shoe horses, do leatherwork, hunt and enjoy the outdoors, shoot guns and most of all spend time with his family.

Becoming A Cowboy Poet

According to Skylar, "When I was young I read some cowboy poetry books that my Dad had and just started writing my own because I enjoyed the humor I found in them."

What makes being a cowboy so ingrained in your life that it leads you to poetry?

Skylar relates, "I wouldn't consider myself a cowboy but I enjoy the rural lifestyle. I'm quite conservative which is one thing I often express in my poetry."

Who is my favorite cowboy poet?

"I'm a fan of many other cowboy poets but a couple of my favorites are definitely Don Kennington and Waddie Mitchell," says Skylar.

What inspires you about Marless' artwork?

Skylar discusses, "Marless is an unbelievably talented artist whose paintings are very lifelike and detailed. Every painting tells many stories in itself and us as poets have been privileged enough to choose the stories we see in them and write them down."

One thing I want to share in my poetry?

"I want people to laugh when they read or hear my poetry because I like to make people smile. In my poems that are more serious or less humorous, I want to get people thinking and their wheels spinning in their own heads as they relate to my poetry in different ways," believes Skylar.

One Great Ride and with Whom?

"I like to ride on the mountain, but any riding I do with my wife and kids is a great day of riding. I also enjoy riding with my Dad, Greg Harwood, who also has had poems accepted for this book," reveals Skylar.

Slim McWilliams

About Slim McWilliams

"I am part of the fifth generation of our family born in Colorado. My first paying job was working for my uncle on his ranch in Wyoming. I worked on ranches from Montana to Arizona, riding rough string, working cattle, and guiding both pack trips and hunters," says Slim.

Slim continues, "From there I followed a logical career path. I drove truck, irrigated, worked road construction, taught school, worked as a grease monkey, rodeoed, worked as a carpenter, sold potato chips, was a musician, worked on drilling rigs, trained horses, and was a banker. (Not everyone can earn an honest living his whole life)," jokes Slim.

Becoming A Cowboy Poet

According to Slim, "When I was three years old I got a wind up phonograph and some 78 rpm records with cowboy songs on them. I was hooked. Working as a cowboy, I tried to learn the original versions of all the authentic old time cowboy songs. While guiding pack trips I had a lot of time in the saddle and I started to put together songs about people I knew and incidents I witnessed. I follow the maxim, "Never let a little lie stand in the way of a good story."

What makes being a cowboy so ingrained in your life that it leads you to poetry?

"Most cowboys observe life from a different perspective than normal folks do. For example, we enjoy a good wreck; someone getting his head stuck in the dirt by a salty bronc, getting freight-trained by a ringy cow, or getting treed by a moose. Of course, we enjoy it even more if we get to watch the wreck happen instead of participating," answered Slim.

Slim says, "Once you've witnessed or participated in such events, you enjoy sharing them with anyone who will listen and enjoy them. Some cowboys have a real talent for poetry and songs."

Who is your favorite cowboy poet?

Slim laughs, "There are so many excellent poets out there! Poets such as Chris Issacs, Vess Quinlan, and Mike Dunn, Waddie Mitchell, Nona Carver Kelly, Sam DeLeeuw, and a herd of others!"

What inspires you about Marless' artwork?

"Her picture, 'Mischief' is fascinating because it shows five cowboys out on a typical southwest range. The cowboys are side by side, sittin' on their spurs and looking out in front of them. Behind them are three horses. And between the five cowboys, only one has a rope. The incongruities of five cowboys out in cow country with only three horses and one rope between them begs the questions, "What happened before this scene?" "What mischief were they up to?" wonders Slim.

What is the one thing you want to share with people in your poetry?

Slim states, "I like to share the West as it really was and the way it really is today. The privilege of living this life in this country – sharing the fun and the pain – testing yourself – and being so thankful that our Creator saw fit to create cowboys and the Rocky Mountain West along with the rest of creation."

If you could take one great ride, who would it be with and where would you go?

"I'd love to take my wife, Sue, and a couple of pack horses and start where Eagle Creek joins the North Fork of the Shoshone River on the west edge of Yellowstone Park. After a long winding trip, we'd end up going down Deer Creek to the South Fork of the Shoshone River. I'd sure like to see that country one more time!" relays Slim.

GARY PENNEY

About Gary Penney

As with most writers, life has its way of showing you a path of lessons. So it has been with poet Gary Penney. Gary was raised in the small town of Corsicana, Texas but spent most weekends on his grandparents' farms where he loved being around and interacting with livestock.

Gary's love for the country life lead him to became an active member of FFA in high school and then on to earn a B.S. degree in Agriculture from Sam Houston State University. Gary spent 10 years in the turkey industry prior to joining M&M/Mars Candy Company as a quality technician. With a career spanning over 30 years with Mars, Gary spent the final eight years prior to his retirement as the Lead Sensory Technician / Taste Trainer (Head candy taster).

Let's just say those must have been the sweetest eight years of all.

Becoming A Cowboy Poet

As luck would have it for all of us, a Cowboy Poet friend of Gary's introduced him to the art of Cowboy Poetry in 2004 by asking Gary to write a poem for him. According to Gary, "I was taken aback! I wrote the poem and listened to him perform it. After that I was hooked. I began learning the old favorites and then I began writing poems on my own. Now I conduct my own performances of both old favorites and original poetry, usually at retirement centers or churches. I much prefer performing to writing."

What makes being a cowboy so ingrained in your life that it leads you to poetry?

According to Gary, "Everyone loves a cowboy. Many folks dream of being a cowboy. Unfortunately, that reality is not to be for most of us in these days and times. However, I can make that dream somewhat come to life on paper or recitation in the beautiful prose of a poem. Cowboys and cowboy life will always live in the hearts of those who dream it."

Who is your favorite cowboy poet?

Gary quips, "I don't really have one favorite because each poet brings something different to the table."

What inspires you about Marless' artwork?

"Marless brings a wide variety of subjects to the canvas. In people and animals – the facial expressions make you wonder what has led up to this point. Postures accentuate situations or add mystery. Colors add to the mood. Backgrounds make me wonder of the locations. All of these lend themselves to help me write a story about what I see," says Gary.

What is the one thing you want to share with people in your poetry?

"LIFE and how great it is. Life is not always fair, but you CAN play with the hand you are dealt. Smile and feel good about LIFE," spoken like a true cowboy Gary Penney.

One Great Ride and with Whom?

Gary says, "I would love to ride through the Fall Aspens of Colorado with Roy and Dale. They were more than just Silver Screen Cowboys. They lived the life, loved animals, loved kids, and loved God. And, they could sing great Western songs. I believe that's why they are so endeared to so many folks my age. They were real."

Gary Penney ★ pennegar@hotmail.com

RICHARD WRIGHT

About Richard Wright
Spending the long and beautiful summers amid the farms and ranches in Salinas Valley in California helped to develop the love of the cowboy, the horse and the wide-open spaces. At age 19, Richard joined the U.S. Air Force, making it a career and retiring after 20 years. According to Richard, "I've traveled extensively, having been to 44 of our states and 18 countries. I currently live in Spring, Texas and though not born here, consider myself Texan through and through."

Becoming a Cowboy Poet
Richard has always written many forms of poetry over the years, but it was growing up in the West and living in so many great western towns, like Cheyenne, Bozeman, and Alamogordo, that drew him to write Cowboy Poetry. "There's something pure and honest about poetry. I love the themes of the West, nature, and basic relationships. I value its unpretentious tone," says Richard.

What makes being a cowboy so ingrained in your life that it leads you to poetry?
Spoken like a true Cowboy, Richard says it best, "Being a cowboy is a state of mind as much as a way of life. It's about how you carry yourself, how you treat others, and living your life with a code of honor. Those are the things that inspire my poems."

Who is your favorite Cowboy poet?
With a love for the dramatic, Richard says, "I'm quite fond of Wallace McRae's writing. I enjoy his humor and also his passion for the cowboy life. I also enjoy Fin Bayles. 'The Death of Juan Chacon' is one of my favorite poems in any form – devastatingly real and horribly tragic!"

What inspires you about Marless Fellows' artwork?
"Of course the subject matter of the West grabs me right away! If you look deeper, however, you'll see feeling in her paintings. It may be a weary cowboy, a playful horse, or the love of a western vista. I love that about Marless – what she cares about comes across in her paintings," says Richard.

What is the one thing you want to share with people in your poetry?
"Relationships. Even when there are no people in my poems, there are still relationships represented. Nothing lives on this Earth without relationships. I enjoy capturing those within a western setting," states Richard.

If you could take one great ride, who would it be with and where would you go?
Who doesn't dream of one great ride, Richard would take one filled with memories. "It would be with my wife and my sister and her husband, from Cloudcroft to Ruidoso in New Mexico – beautiful country! If I could go back in time, it would be with John Wayne across Monument Valley...hey, maybe an idea for a future poem!"

Richard Wright ★ rawright7738@gmail.com

COWBOY'S JOURNAL